WORKING
TERRIERS

WORKING TERRIERS

MARK GILES

HUDDLESFORD PUBLICATIONS

Huddlesford Publications
Hawthorn House
Bowdell Lane
Brookland
Kent TN29 9RW

First published 1988
© Mark Giles

British Library Cataloguing in Publication Data
Giles, Mark
  Working terriers.
  1. Working terriers
  I. Title
  636.7'55

ISBN 0–907827–10–1

CE

636.7

C2 124261 99

Set by R. H. Services, Welwyn, Hertfordshire
Printed and bound by Biddles Ltd, Guildford and Kings Lynn

Contents

Introduction

I HOPE YOU WILL enjoy reading this book which I have written not as a professional author of books – which I certainly am not as before this postcards and letters were the limit of my literary ambitions – but as an owner of working terriers and lurchers, someone who keeps his dogs because they are working dogs and for no other purpose. You do not get any rosettes working your terriers, just the self-satisfaction that goes with owning, training and working a terrier. There are setbacks, disappointments and heartaches, as in almost all sports which involve working dogs, but an older and more enjoyable sport would be very hard to find.

I have drawn on my friends' and my own experiences of rearing, owning and training working terriers and if by reading this book you gain some pieces of information or a few useful tips you can put to use when next working your terriers or when fetching up your next pup, then my efforts will not have been in vain. I hope you will get some practical use out of this book as well as an enjoyable read.

I hope you will find in the following pages a picture of the working terrier scene as it is today and that reading this book will add in some small part at least to your enjoyment of keeping and working your terriers.

Mark Giles 1988

All shapes, sizes and colours. Given the chance most will work.

—1—

Terrier Breeds and Crosses

BEFORE DISCUSSING THE various types of terrier there are one or two general points that seem worth making.

The fact is it does not matter if you work a border, Jack Russell, lakeland/patterdale or any other kind of terrier, they should all have the same thing in common if they come from working stock – their love of working fox underground. Also it does not matter if they are black, red, grizzle, black and white or any other colour, so far as their working ability is concerned. You could choose any one of the breeds I shall mention but the most popular terrier breeds used by terriermen today, and the best choice for a working terrier, are border, Jack Russell, patterdale, lakeland or fell-type terrier, or a cross of any two of these breeds. It is a pity that some of the other terrier breeds have slipped out of use (such as Sealyham, Dandy Dinmont, fox terrier, cairn, Welsh terrier) but these terrier breeds are no longer bred for the purpose we want a terrier for, and they are now used just for walking around a Kennel Club show ring and nothing else. Most have had all their working instinct bred out of them.

Remember fighting another dog does not prove any terrier's courage. Some dogs will fight, even kill, other terriers and then shy away from going to ground to face a fox. I have had two border terrier stud dogs and two Jack Russell studs: and all were being used on bitches regularly, but all four of them could be worked together and worked to rat and fox without fighting or quarrelling at all. That is something to be proud of when looking for temperament and is something which is quite often neglected among a lot of would-be terriermen of today, I am sorry to say. Few terriers will back away from a fight and I would not expect any of my terriers not to retaliate when attacked, but I always, and I do not mind repeating myself on this subject, I always check my terriers for fighting or trying to provoke a fight. I never have trouble with my border terrier bitches, they all seem to mix without quarrelling, and even my Jack Russell bitches seem to enjoy the company of other terriers.

Entering a terrier into an earth.

If you own terriers and do not work them, or if you own them for showing and breeding purposes only, but would like to see if they still have the instinct to work, then seek out a reputable terrierman, a man without biased views on terriers. Ask him if you can accompany him with one, or maybe two, of your terriers. Whether they be Sealyhams, fox terriers, Dandies, cairns, borders, lakelands, Scotties or any other kind, try them at some foxhunting, he may even, if you wish, take a youngster and enter it for you. If more people did this then our terriers would have a little bit more of a chance of surviving the Kennel Club's test of time, which as often as not destroys the dog's true working abilities, and perhaps more show breeders would be encouraged to take working ability as well as looks into consideration in their breeding programmes.

THE MOST POPULAR WORKING TERRIERS OF TODAY

The Jack Russell Terrier
Many Jack Russells today have been labelled by quite a few terriermen as gutless and cowardly but in my experience most of the men who state this are hardened lakeland terrier owners. Men who own dogs that thrash the life out of a fox without batting an eyelid, and buy a Jack Russell and expect it to do the same thing as a lakeland. Some Russells will kill foxes – we have one which will kill foxes without making a sound and is as hard as the toughest patterdale or lakeland fell-type terrier. However, that is not what they have been used for in the south and not what most terriermen in the south of England, or the part of the country where I work terriers, want them for. In fact a Jack Russell of about 12 inches which will go to ground, find its quarry and bay like mad is my kind of terrier.

But nine out of ten Jack Russells today (and this probably applies to all terriers) do not see serious earth work to fox. If you breed litters of terriers and two pups out of every litter end up as workers then you are doing very well indeed. Most will be bought as fox workers and end up ratting and rabbiting, or just as pets. Some people are too scared to work their terrier for fear of getting them too badly hurt, or even killed, by going to ground at a fox.

Where Russells are concerned some people see a tri-coloured Jack Russell working, like what they see and go out and buy a tri-coloured puppy thinking that if it is the same colour then it

11

Beagle, the author's Jack Russell terrier, baying at his quarry towards the end of the dig.

will work the same. But they couldn't be more wrong, as colour has no bearing on working ability and it is potential and not looks that should influence your decision when buying.

If you have a Russell-type bitch of the small game type don't go mad and breed her to even smaller Jack Russell dogs. If you keep breeding too small then your dogs will end up with jaws that are far too small and weak to tackle a fox. I have a Jack Russell bitch, nine inches at the shoulder, smooth-coated, which I put to my own dog, Beagle, who is about 12 inches. The puppies out of these two should vary from 9–12 inches at the shoulder which is an ideal height for working underground, as did the last litter. The type of terrier that follows at the heels of Bert Gripton in Phil Drabble's book *Of Pedigree Unknown* is sadly a type which seems to be disappearing, as the show Jack Russell is becoming more popular and so smarter dogs are being bred. Don't get me wrong though, I am all in favour of a smarter Jack Russell and I wouldn't deliberately breed an ugly terrier just for the sake of it, but I do believe in breeding worker to worker. I confess that I have, in the past, used border terrier blood to smarten up my own Jack Russells to a more even type of terrier.

Jack Russells come in many shapes and sizes, rough and smooth.

Some of the Jack Russells which are bred (I call them Jack Russells but really they are nothing like the Rev. Jack's dogs at all) are more like small bassets without the long hound-like ears and long tail, and that's only because their tails are docked at three to four days old. Some of the terriers that I have seen are really heavily coloured and marked, almost the same as the basset hound. I do believe that the basset hound contributed a great deal to the make-up of most of the little short bow-legged terriers seen today. I also believe the Beagle played a large part in the make-up – which is why I named my Jack Russell dog Beagle. He is the same colour as a beagle and throws his tongue whilst following a scent. Also, without doubt, there has been a bit

13

of bull terrier added somewhere along the lines, for most of those little short-legged terriers boast a large bull terrier-type head. Some even have those little bull terrierish squinty, reddish eyes, which tell you straight away that there's a dash of old English Bull Terrier in their ancestry. This blood gives them not only a powerful head and jaw and limitless courage but also a large and powerful chest, which is frowned upon by most terriermen in the south of England. However, some of the dogs seen today at working terrier shows are looking a little bit more like the old type of Jack Russell terrier of yesteryear.

A noted worker, small but with a big heart.

Don't make the common mistake and disregard the small short-legged Jack Russell terriers – those with old-fashioned bowed Queen Anne legs. I have used this type of terrier many times and haven't found any fault in them at all where working ability is concerned. In fact the only drawback you might find is that you will not win any shows or rosettes with them but if you are only looking for a terrier to do a job of work then it doesn't really matter does it? Many of the old working terriers of yesteryear were of this type, some of them were amongst the ugliest dogs that I have ever seen, but when they were doing a job of work they were little darlings who were, and in my mind still are, treasures of the working terrier scene. Although they are a far cry from what the famous Reverend Jack Russell bred and worked, and for looks he most likely wouldn't have given them house-room, I think he would today rather have one of those ugly little workers than a smart show fox terrier which does not have the heart to go to ground and face a fox in his earth.

Derek Hume's Jack Russell dog Grip.

15

At some of the working terrier shows that I have been to in recent months I have seen some really nice looking Russells with good straight, long legs, narrow chests that can easily be spanned around the ribcage by a man's or woman's hands. If you cannot span a terrier around his ribs he will be of little use as an earth dog. I think some of the smart-looking terriers owe their good looks to either a dash of lakeland or border terrier in their ancestry. I have seen some really smart-looking Russells put together which have thrown puppies that look more like street accidents, rather than purpose-bred working terriers. So, it's a good idea to see the parents of the terrier puppy to get an idea what kind of terrier your choice of puppy will be but don't take it for granted that your puppy will turn out to be a carbon copy of its parents. You may find out that one of your puppy's parents has a grandmother or uncle that's as ugly and as useless as a bucket of coal and your puppy could turn out to be a direct throwback to dear old uncle or grandmother. Even in the best strains of terrier one pops up now and again, if their owners would only admit it.

The author's Jack Russells Midge and his daughter Meg.

Most farms in my area boast two or three Jack Russells, all of different types, kept for keeping down vermin or owned by sporting farmers who keep them for bushing, and I have acquired a few of their pups from time to time. Given half a chance most of them work OK and it has been, in my experience and of most terriermen in the south, that most Jack Russells from a working line, if entered properly, have been excellent workers. It is certainly true that they all have a keen instinct to hunt, and from my own experience to hunt anything.

Tammy, a Jack Russell bitch to be proud of.

Some Jack Russells can also be as temperamental as the border terrier to enter. I think this is why a lot of terriermen today have gone over to the lakeland terrier as a breed. It is very hard to ruin a lakeland by lots of noise and shouting. Some Russells and most borders have to be entered very carefully as lots of noise and shouting will ruin some terriers which would otherwise be excellent workers. In my very early years of terrier work I ruined some excellent young border terriers by constant picking up, by being noisy and by shouting to them whilst they worked. A noisy, loud, shouting person will be of little use to a border terrier or Jack Russell terrier of timid nature.

Slim Farmer, who is a past master at entering terriers, has successfully entered to fox and badger (when badger digging was legal practice for terriermen) Norfolk, Norwich Terriers and also West Highland White Terriers, all of which saw hunt service and serious earth work and acquitted themselves to fox and badgers. They were particularly good on foxes that had been run to ground by foxhounds and, believe me, a fox that has been run to ground by foxhounds is a match for any terrier and will punish any terrier far more than a fox which has been found lying up in an earth.

I'm not going to pretend to be any judge of show terriers, I have never judged a terrier show, nor would I like to. In fact the only judging that I do is to choose a working terrier which suits me and the country that I hunt. That, plus my own experience of going to shows and hearing some of the stick that some of the judges take from sore losers convinced, before they got into the showring, that they should have been placed 1st makes me think that I wouldn't like the job at all, and I don't think that I would ever accept the arduous task of judging a terrier or lurcher show.

The Border Terrier
The border terrier had a set standard laid down by its owners, breeders and workers when it was accepted by the Kennel Club as a pure breed. This was a most excellent standard which most terrier breeders would do well to try and keep to, as it states quite clearly that the border terrier is essentially a working terrier and that it would be able to follow horse and hound, and can combine activity with gameness. It should have a head and skull like an otter with dark nose and dark, alert, eyes; ears should be small, V-shaped, not over-thick and they should drop close down to the cheek; teeth should have a scissor-like grip and the top teeth should be just in front of the lower, and not undershot (where the front lower-teeth stick out in front of the rest of the mouth); neck of moderate length, forequarters and forelegs straight and not too heavy-boned; body deep and narrow and fairly long; ribs carried well back and not over-sprung and should be able to be spanned by both hands behind the shoulder; feet small with thick pads; tail not too short, fairly thick at the base and then tapering down to an almost carrot shape, but *not carried* over the back in a round, curled fashion; coat harsh and dense with close undercoat and a good thick skin; colour – red, wheaten, grizzle, tan or blue and tan; weight and size – dogs between 13–15½ pounds, bitches

A keen looking border bitch.

between 11½–14 pounds. This precise standard was laid down to try to keep the border terrier a working terrier as well as a potential show winner. Also, according to that very fine and enjoyable book called *The Border Terrier* by Anne Roslin-

19

Williams the border terrier standard is also the blueprint for producing the type of terrier to follow horse and hound to hunt and work foxes in Northumberland. But even this strain of terrier has some funny looking specimens turn up.

I have bred some really odd-shaped borders, some of them looking like shockmuzzled little furry gremlins, with so many face furnishings that you would not take them to be a working terrier, but more like Mrs Pumphries' Tricky Woo from the series *All Creatures Great and Small*. I have also bred, from borders that were, to be quite honest, as ugly as sin some that have become cracking show types for their owners and that have won many shows. Where face furnishings are concerned it doesn't matter if your border, or any other kind of terrier for that matter, has as many whiskers and as much hair around its face as any other kind of dog. Once you start working your terrier and it's going to ground the earth, soil and clay will strip out most of your dog's coat and if your terrier starts getting bitten around the face and cheek, chances are most of the furnishings will be chewed off; giving him that more pointed-looking face. He may

Note the border terrier's heavy waterproof coat.

even lose his proud border terrier beard which most owners love to brush and groom to keep it knot-free.

Although the border terrier standard states that dogs should weigh between 13–15½ pounds, my old border dog Toby is about 19 pounds and most of the border terriers that you see at shows today are somewhere around 17–19 pounds. Many of them are getting very fiery and vicious which is not like the breed should be, for one of the things which first attracted me to the border terrier was its good temperament and ability to get on with its fellow canines, not wanting to fight all the time to prove its toughness. The border terrier has never had to prove its toughness or gameness by fighting other dogs, it's always proved itself by facing its quarry, underground for as long as it takes.

A border terrier puppy taken on a dig to see what goes on as part of its early training.

The border terrier is at the moment taking a bit of a bashing in the working scene and a few terriermen are starting to breed for good looks rather than for workers. What puts most people off the border terrier is its tendency to be a slow entering terrier. I feel that I should point out that there are strains of border which enter as easily as any other kind of terrier, but they do vary quite a lot. Many of my border terrier bitch Trixy's pups enter very easily and by the time that they are a year old they are working fox.

If you haven't had a border terrier, or if you are starting up in the terrier world and haven't had a working terrier before and you wish to start with a border terrier, don't buy from the very first advert that you see, buy from a well-known worker. Don't make the mistake of going to a working terrier show and buy or order a puppy from the best show winner or best looker. If the best looker and show winner is also a regular worker, seeing work every week during hunting months, then by all means buy one, but if they don't work or haven't worked then don't buy a puppy from them. Save your money and spend it with someone who takes as much pride, or more, in working his border as he does showing them. Don't listen to stories of border terriers being soft because they most certainly are not.

Border terriers of about 1900.

Through the years the border has been smartened up. In C. G. E. Wimhurst's *The Book on Terriers* (an excellent book which shows terriers today and also as they were), there are two photos opposite page 32, one photo of Miss B Eccles's champion border dog 'Chalcroft the Card', holder of a MFH Working Certificate. A smart-looking show-winning worker, truly a rare dog. Another photo shows five rather rougher looking borders of about 1900, with quite a lot of that thick, tough, outdoor coat that gives them all the protection they need from rain, snow and the rough climate in their native north. A very interesting article in one of the *Working Terrier Year Books* about the border terrier states that, more or less, the border terrier would do well to follow the example of the lakeland terrier which is at present split into two – the show lakeland and the working non-registered fell lakeland and, for want of a better term, go their own way, as did the fell lakeland. I am doing just that – keeping my borders pure but just breeding worker to worker, putting aside looks for working ability and, sin-of-sins, now I don't even bother to Kennel Club register them. They might look a bit rough and ready, and scruffy but they do what's asked of them above and below ground. I know I might be criticised for this and people might even say that I will cross the border with other strains of working terriers, but that shall never happen. I shall keep my borders pure and keep records of each puppy's sire and dam, and just breed worker to worker and see what happens. You never know I might even breed a working border terrier that's good enough to win a show in years to come.

A border terrier proving its ability as a ratting dog.

The Lakeland/Patterdale Terrier
The Lake District is probably one of England's most picturesque places and also one of its most harsh and dangerous. Most of the men who live there are keen sportsmen and it's no wonder that a rough and ready type of terrier came about. A good weatherproof coat is an asset to any terrier, whether he works

A keen looking lakeland showing the typical workmanlike expression common to the breed.

north or south. Although in the south of England a smooth-coated dog can take most of our rough weather, a good thick coat is always desirable.

It seems that at the moment there's a difference of opinion whether the so-called patterdale is in fact a lakeland or whether it is a separate and distinct type. Personally I think patterdales and lakelands are two different types of northern working terriers. There are terriermen, of course, who deny this saying, there is no such thing as a patterdale terrier, the patterdale being just a smooth-coated version of the lakeland terrier, but I do not agree with this. I find most strains of what are referred to as patterdales will stand back and bay but lakelands do not have the discretion of some patterdales, just that blind lakeland courage we all have come to know and love. To me a patterdale is a smooth-coated northern working terrier with a bull terrier type head.

Two of Brian Nuttall's famous patterdale pups.

Some of the lakelands that I have seen have been ever so tall with narrow chests. I have seen some red and black and tan lakelands as tall as whippets and, surprisingly, all leg. One of them I could span easily and it was well over 14½ inches, perhaps even more, at the shoulder. But legs can be folded up and I suppose the dogs can manage most earths and drains. Why they came to be so tall, I suppose, was to follow hounds across the rugged northern hills and mountains. One theory was that the lakeland's job was to enter, kill the fox or bolt him for the hounds to run. Another theory was that the terrier was to find the fox which hounds had marked to ground, tackle him and cripple him somewhat so that when he finally bolted the hounds could catch him easily. Personally I do not hold with this school of thought.

The author's very game patterdale bitch Tammy.

Mind you, I pity any fox which is on the other end of one of those terriers. If you intend to keep a lot of lakelands you will have to be careful about kennelling them together because lakeland terriers are the very worst for fighting. In my own experience nine out of ten kennel fights occur between hunting trips and I wouldn't advise kennelling more than two lakelands together. Even two can be difficult if one is much larger than the other. For instance, say you have a lakeland bitch 12 inches at the shoulder, kennelled with a 14–15 inch dog, both of whom are just a bit quarrelsome, and a fight breaks out – it's odds on who is going to win. Lakelands don't fight for fun, when they fight they mean it and don't back away. So try and keep kennels equal, by that I mean if you have four lakelands, or for that matter any other kind of terrier, and have two big dogs about 14½ inches at the shoulder and two bitches at 12 inches at the shoulder, kennel the two 14 inch dogs together and the two bitches together. If they are too bad, kennel them singly.

A young patterdale bitch from Bill Brightmoor's strain, owned by Tony Brown.

Fortunately I have been very lucky with my own lakeland types, they have been very well behaved and I haven't had much trouble with them fighting. In fact they have been very good and quite even-tempered but I have always gone for the patterdale types instead of the more common black and tan ones as I believe them to be more even-tempered. Also for the earths in my area a big leggy type of dog with a hard disposition is at a disadvantage.

This lakeland shows the broad nosed boxy head characteristic of the breed.

Geoffery Sparrow, author of *Terriers' Vocation*, mentioned having difficulty with a large lakeland in my area and I have no doubt that he did for the earths that Sparrow worked are still being used. I work them now and an oversized dog, or for that matter any large lakeland terrier, is at a disadvantage. The only earths a big terrier could be worked in with any success and without danger of getting hurt or trapped are large earths on downlands. But in the lowlands and in the weald of Sussex the sort of lakeland you'd need is a very narrow and small type, about 13 inches at the shoulder at most and not to be overhard. A small lakeland-type terrier that doesn't want to kill every fox that it sees, and will bay a fox, is a very useful terrier for working in the south. In fact the terriermen for both foxhound packs in my district use lakelands and patterdales of this stamp. Geoff, my hunting partner, has recently brought a patterdale bitch from the Chiddingfold and Leconfield Hunt terrierman. Both parents work on the hunt so perhaps this smaller baying type of northern terrier is becoming much more popular. Practically all the would-be terriermen around now own either lakelands or patterdales – it seems that they are the 'in thing' in the south.

Where once it was mostly Russells or borders which were kept now it is lakelands and patterdales. True they are probably the guttsiest of working terrier breeds, for you rarely see a bad or cowardly one, and any hunter who regards a fox as vermin to be killed by a terrier owns one of these dogs. In the south a terrier's job is to bolt a fox for hounds and riders to chase – to kill a fox underground while working for a foxhound pack is a very serious fault and definitely not desired. Yet in the north when hounds have run a fox to ground, a lakeland's job is either to kill it or bolt it. Tremendous stories are told about these dogs and their escapades and hunting ability. One such case is of a friend of mine, from Portsmouth, who owned a very large black and tan lakeland bitch who was scarred from head to tail. When my friend had first purchased her from Lambourn Lurcher Show, in the early 1980s, she was about two-years-old and only just entered to earth work. Her new owner took her back to Portsmouth and the very next day, he took his new terrier out to try her at a fox. She was put to ground on a large sandbank where the earth was known to be deep at one end and shallow at the other end. She had no locator on but only after a few seconds

29

of entering the earth she could be heard making contact with her fox. One fox bolted but the bitch could still be heard mixing it with her fox. Her owner and friends decided to dig to her and they got nearer to her, the quieter she became. By the time the diggers broke through into the tunnel the only thing that they found was a very dead fox. They listened for a while and could hear her making contact with another fox so the diggers began to tunnel in to her but it seemed that she was going in further. After about six hours digging night had fallen and torches were sent for.

A beautiful pair of red lakelands.

By midnight they had dug a huge chunk out of the bank and thought it best to leave it until daylight. All the holes were blocked and when they returned next morning they found them all unblocked, but no sign of the bitch could be seen or heard. Another terrier was entered, one which would bay and mark well and after disappearing down the tunnel she could be heard baying loudly. After another long spell of digging they reached the new terrier, who was pulled out. One of the diggers shone a torch into the tube and the rear end of a fox could be seen. The fox was pulled out – he had been dead for a very long time. Just behind the dead fox was the Lakeland bitch, alive and a little cramped. She had killed her second fox and got stuck behind him, as the hole was quite narrow. The bitch was taken home and given some special care, and was ready to go again the very next weekend, when she proved herself yet again. For courage and game working ability the lakeland terrier is hard to beat.

A border and lakeland, dogs with very different temperaments.

The border terrier and the lakeland come from the same part of the country, but their temperaments and characters are totally different. Where some strains of border can be entered to fox and will stand off and bay the lakeland, instead of standing back and baying at his quarry, tries to rush in and finish it off. Out of all the pure-bred lakelands that I have seen, I have rarely seen one that would stand off and bay his fox. Even the ones we have had were terrifically hard. If you do get one that will stand off and bay then you will have a working terrier worth having.

Black fell type terriers are reputedly very hard.

The Fell Terrier

Personally I like the northern working terriers such as lakelands, patterdales, border terriers and the fell-types, which quite often show a great deal of Bedlington terrier blood in their breeding. Most have a sign of the silky Bedlington topknot on their heads and in their coat. I think the so-called fell terrier-types seen at most terrier shows have come into being by crossing the border, Bedlingtons, lakeland and patterdale-types together, producing a terrier with the lakeland temperament and the longer Bedlington's body and thick silky Bedlington coat. Some even have a border terrier-looking head. Some of the photos that I have seen of the great Tommy Dobson and his dogs have been with dogs that have more Bedlington influence than anything else. I think a northern terrier needs a large, heavy water and weatherproof coat to help keep out the harsh Cumbrian winters and frosts. Some of the old border terriers, such as the ones on page 37 in that fine book *Border Tales*, shows a group of Mr W Barton's terriers taken in 1915. It is a group of five terriers, some of which show a sign of the silky topknot and silky-type coat of the Bedlington. Even some of my own borders show signs of that same silky topknot and even the silky coat. I personally like this long silky coat in the border terrier.

From this you can see that fell terrier types are very variable in looks, but the one thing they have in common is courage though they are not normally as hard as the lakeland.

THE LESS POPULAR WORKING TERRIERS OF TODAY

Today there are three main types of working terrier – the Jack Russell, border and lakeland/patterdale but it is interesting to stop and look for a moment at some of the other types of terriers that used to be worked but are now rarely seen outside the show ring. At one time most terriers were used as workers and could give good account of themselves against fox or badger, but where have they gone today? All ruined by the craze for breeding for looks and not working ability. I have said it before, and no doubt I will say it again, the Kennel Club has a lot to answer for, and when you are deciding on a mating for your terrier remember to breed worker to worker and turn your back on breeding for good looks only, else there will be very few working terriers left.

Famous breeds like the Sealyham, Bedlington and dachshund and perhaps less well-known breeds such as the Dandie Dinmont and Norwich terrier all were known workers at one time.

33

The Fox Terrier

In 1872 when the wire fox terrier first appeared on the show ring scene at Birmingham I think it still had the appearance of a true working terrier, and from old records and photos that I have seen its coat looked hard, thick and straight, unlike the present day fox terrier which has a softer, more curly coat than its ancestors. There are fearsome accounts of wire fox terriers of old – accounts of great working ability above and below ground. One such account is of a wire fox terrier called Powderham Jack who was entered in a large badger sett one midday and began baying and chasing the badger around its sett. Another terrier was sent in to help him but after a time came out quite bedgraggled. When night began to fall Powderham Jack crawled out badly bitten, and scarred around the face and neck. He had been to ground for six hours and was in quite a bad way. The old account of this goes on to say that the next day the sett was found to hold two badgers, one was bagged alive and unharmed, the other was dead and weighed 26 lbs. At the time it was thought that old Powderham Jack had killed the brock but personally I think it died of heart failure. Nevertheless, the wire fox terrier worried it to a state whereby it did have heart failure.

Fox terriers of old could rub shoulders with the gamest of them all. Though the smooth fox terrier became a show dog some eight or nine years before the wire-haired fox terrier, neither one in the days circa 1868–1872 was considered worthy of the name fox terrier unless he could prove himself by facing a fox or badger underground. The terriermen of old had no time for a dog unless he was able to work his quarry. What a pity the fox terrier breeders of years gone by haven't passed their love of a good honest working fox terrier on to the breeders of today.

I have in my possession an old print called 'Not at Home' with a polecat coming out of a rabbit warren with three smart-looking, very workman-like fox terriers of that time positioned around the hole waiting for a rabbit, or perhaps even a rat, to bolt. They are much thicker in the body and have much heavier jaws than we are used to though they are without a doubt smooth fox terriers. The artist was Frank Patton, and the print is dated 1887, about the time Buffalo Bill brought his Wild West Show to England. I mention this because there are small sketches around the edge of the print depicting Buffalo Bill's

Wild West Rodeo Show, so perhaps our artist was a cowboy fan as well as being keen on terriers. The nicest fox terrier bitch I have seen in the 1980s was on a chicken farm not far from my home. She's a smooth-coated bitch, the traditional red and white colour, and was kept as a family pet and to help keep down rats on the farm, at which she was first class. Even when she had a bad accident with a combine harvester and lost her front left paw she didn't stop catching rats.

A fox terrier of the 1870s.

I think that there are strains of fox terriers being bred, both wire-haired and smooth, which look as if they could do a job of work when it comes to hunting fox, rats and rabbits. Who knows, perhaps one day I might try one, in my own kennels. I hear that Bert Gripton has a fox terrier that works quite well and he has mated it to his Jack Russell bitches, and produced some useful workers. Perhaps they are catching on again and other terriermen may use them with the result that there will be a growing number of genuine working fox terriers around again instead of just the show bred variety.

Irish Terriers

The Irish breeds such as the Kerry Blue or Glen of Imaal, or the Irish Terrier, are fairly rarely seen as workers over here. I have seen a Glen of Imaal working in the south of England, although I must admit he did have to have his earths picked for him, as he was just a bit on the thick, dumpy side. But when he reached his quarry, a gamer, harder dog any terrierman would be hard pushed to find. He had to have a locator collar on constantly when he was to ground because of his muteness, for he just destroyed foxes.

Irish terriers of the 1800s.

I believe there are some Kerry Blues in this country but I must admit I haven't seen one working to date and I am not going to pretend to know a great deal about the breed, because I don't, other than from what I have read in books on terrier breeds. In fact, far too little information is available about the Irish breeds or crosses. Any authorities on the Kerry Blue or Glen of Imaal or any other Irish Terrier breed (before I go any further I should say any working authority, someone who still breeds and works them) would do well to write a book on them; for I know the Irish terriermen are very interested in our British working terriers and I, for one, am more than keenly interested in the Irish working terrier breeds and crosses.

Dachshund

Even the dachshund was once a badger-digging dog, the very word dachshund means badgerhound. From the old photos that I have seen, the old-time working dachshunds were much longer in the leg, had much stronger jaws and more powerful heads. The show bench people have a lot to answer for where working qualities are concerned, because the modern dachshund is far from suitable for constant earth work, being far too short in the leg and long in the body, earning them that old nickname the 'sausage' dog. That long, thin and very often snipey, light jaw and also narrow, small skull makes them unsuitable as a working terrier. Don't rule them out as a bushing or rabbiting dog, they may not be much use as a fox dog but they will, if trained right, work cover and flush out rabbits. If you do, however, go for a dachshund, go for a wire-haired one because they are far more suited for work than the smooth-coated or long silky-haired ones that I have seen. The wire-haired dachshund still has a sporty nature, despite the show benches' bad influence. It has also been crossed with borders, Russells and even lakelands.

Sealyhams

If only there were one third of the people keeping working Sealyhams as there are keeping the show dog variety then we would not have to worry, but I am afraid that it is too late. Perhaps it is our own fault, there are plenty of terriermen willing to keep lakelands, patterdales, borders and Russells but not willing to keep a Sealyham. Perhaps if we had kept on working Sealyhams, keeping them just for ability and not for appearance, we might still have them in our working kennels. It is not entirely the Kennel Club that should take all the blame, perhaps half the blame should fall on the shoulders of the terriermen who have evolved since the days of Sir Jocelyn Lucas.

Working Sealyhams are a very rare sight today; these belong to Morris Richards.

It does seem though that we have neglected all the other breeds just to concentrate on border terriers, lakelands, fell terriers, patterdales and Jack Russells. But let's try to do something about the Sealyham. To anyone who owns a working-type Sealyham dog: do yourself and the rest of the working terrier world a favour – advertise your dog for stud, there must be some working terrier Sealyhams left. Let's hear from their owners, beat your own drums, sing your own dog's working ability praises, for if you don't no one else will and where the Sealyham is concerned the drums are well worth beating, and are very, very long overdue. If the old-type Sealyham could be revived then the working terrier scene would take another turn for the better. You only have to go to any terrier show to see which breeds of terrier dominate the working terrier world.

There are some Jack Russell terriers about which resemble the old-type Sealyham quite a lot, possibly due to the fact that they do have the old Sealyham blood in their veins. Perhaps some of them are even descended from Sir Jocelyn Lucas's Sealyhams, who knows? The old-type of Sealyham's shape and ancestry, and general appearance certainly does attract me to them, and also their abundance of working ability. But that is the Sealyham of years gone by, the nearest thing that I have seen to one of the old-type Sealyhams was at the Crawley and Horsham Hunt Terrier Show, about four years ago. A chap from Epsom had a mixture of border terriers and border Russells, all of which showed signs of having done hard work recently. But in the middle of this mass of terriers was one which seemed to stand out from the crowd. About 13 inches at the shoulder and very rough-haired, all white with only a tan ear. Its owner claimed it to be a Jack Russell but it looked far more like a Sealyham than a Russell, so perhaps there are still one or two floating around. I asked the price of the bitch but its owner was so taken by her that he just wouldn't sell.

Why the Sealyham isn't used today puzzles me. Could it be that in the times during the Second World War, and just after, the owners of these little dogs went absolutely mad on the show scene, turning their backs on the working terrier and neglecting to work their dogs? Or did they decline as a worker because terriermen found them to be lacking in working ability as the years went by? I don't think so. Whatever the reason, it's a crying shame that they did turn into the unworkable dog that they are today, for the show Sealyham is far too heavy and built totally differently to the way it used to be, in fact it is far too unsuitable to go to ground and work, or to take seriously as a working terrier.

Without doubt the terrier worst hit by the non-working fraternity is the Sealyham as they were created to hunt fox, badger and otter by a great old sportsman Captain J. Tucker Edwardes. The Sealyham takes its name from the home of Captain Tucker Edwardes, the estate of Sealyham in Pembrokeshire. What grand dogs those old Sealyhams must have been. Lucas's book *Hunt and Working Terriers*, an all time great work on terriers, tells of great fox and badger digging with Sealyhams and whole packs of working Sealyham terriers hunting otter, fox and badger. Lucas mentions having as many as 13 terriers to ground at once without much trouble with fighting or terriers being pushed into their quarry and being badly hurt. But as Lucas said in his chapter on Sealyhams 'a game dog seldom quarrels for they know there's another end in life'. Of all the Sealyhams that I have seen in recent years I haven't seen any Sealyhams that I would give houseroom to as a worker, for they have all been far too big in the chest and head and none of them could be spanned by a man's hands. The old type of Sealyhams, as seen on old photos, have been very useful looking dogs indeed. They were truly one of the greats of the working terrier scene of their day, but sadly not of today.

The only present day working Sealyhams that I have seen have been in photos in the *Working Terrier Year Book*, Volume 1, 1978, on page 17. There's a photo of two present day working Sealyhams and it's a pleasure to see them. I would rather see two workers of the breed than 200 non-workers of the show bench. I am sorry if I sound prejudiced against the showing fraternity, some of my best friends are Kennel Club judges and do not do much other than show their dogs. Although I am one of those people from the school of thought that states that if it's a working dog then it should do a job of work, I don't ignore showing people and some of their dogs still have working instincts but need developing. What I hate about the Kennel Club is the fact that they change the breeds so much, just as they did the Sealyham. Look at the modern Sealyham and then look at the old Ilmer Sealyhams and you will see why the Kennel Club makes my blood boil with rage!

The Bedlington

Take two photos, one of the Bedlington Terrier of today and the other of the Bedlington Terrier of 75 years ago, and you will probably start to wonder what went wrong. What happened to change such a game, intelligent and hardy dog, owned by hard and tough working north country sportsmen, of years gone by into the showy example seen today?

Here is a classic example of people getting on to the scent of that well known quarry the rosette and to catch it what did they do? Well, it was quite simple really, all they had to do was to breed dogs for looks instead of for working ability to take fox, rats and badger.

A nineteenth century Bedlington.

What a hard dog it looked – as game as they come. But now, instead of being a working terrier adding courage and toughness to different strains of terrier, it is best known for producing Bedlington cross greyhounds or Bedlington cross whippets for lamping and ferreting. There are still a few breeders up and down the country who work their dogs, and I believe there is a club called 'The Working Bedlington Terrier Club'. A club like this could do wonders for restoring the Bedlington Terrier to the working scene. But I would advise such a club to go for quality, not quantity and to build a membership of genuine men who want to own a working Bedlington and not those who just want to be a member of the club so as to advertise litter after litter of pups at a good price with no intention of breeding a working Bedlington or even of

41

working one at all. Stay on the right tracks and breed only workers to workers and you will not go far wrong. As I have said about other rare working breeds, beat your own drum. No one will want to keep a Bedlington as a worker unless they think that some one else is working them.

Judy, a working type Bedlington terrier.

Although the origin of the breed is believed to be the Rothbury Forest in Northumberland, in fact it is named after the village of Bedlington, famed for turning out our game working terriers in years gone by.

Cairn, West Highland White, Norfolk and Norwich Terriers

Cairn terriers in principal are just a prick-eared version of the Norfolk and Norwich Terrier, although I have seen Cairns which were a lot bigger than even the biggest Norfolk or Norwich. Some of the photos I have seen of modern-day working cairns have been of really massive looking dogs.

Whether or not the dogs looked big because of the thick heavy coat which they have I do not know, but among people who work cairns they seem to like the big ones in preference to the smaller type.

I must admit if I had to choose between cairn, Norfolk or Norwich, I would go for a Norfolk athough it is believed that a Norwich and a Norfolk have the same temperament. Until 1964 the Kennel Club of England considered the two dogs to be of the same breed and only decided in 1964 that because the Norwich terrier has pricked ears and the Norfolk has drop ears, similar to the border terrier, to call them two different breeds. In the United States the Norwich and the Norfolk are known as the same breed – Norfolk Terriers. It seems that our Yankee neighbours are not so fussy on names as long as the breed works well and the fact that one dog's ears are carried up and the other down does not signify that they are separate breeds.

The pedigree Norfolk or Norwich is a small dog of around 10 to 10½ inches at the shoulder and they come in three colours: red, grizzle and black and tan. The black and tan is most favoured in America as a worker. The Norwich and Norfolk have docked tails, often docked very short which I think spoils its appearance a little. The cairn, in fact, does not have its tail docked and I believe the cairn, Norwich, Norfolk and border terriers have got the same ancestor somewhere in their make up. I do think the Norfolk and Norwich breeders would do well to take a leaf from the cairn and border's books and keep the tails.

The cairn's standard states that they can be a shade smaller than the Norfolk, between nine and 10 inches at the shoulder. I believe the cairns of years ago were great little workers as the very name cairn means the large heap of rocks where foxes and vermin take refuge, and the little dogs took their name because they were expected to follow the foxes and vermin to ground in these large rock earths and deal with them accordingly. Sir Jocelyn Lucas's book *Hunt and Working Terriers* has some photos of some fine looking cairns, Norfolk and Norwich Terriers.

Another breed which evolved through the cairn is the West Highland White Terrier. It is slightly bigger than the cairn – about 11 inches at the shoulder – and is believed to be bred from the white pups of cairn terriers. These were bred until the dog evolved into a distinct breed that threw only pure white pups but kept practically all the cairn characteristicts and I know of modern day Westies being entered to fox with great success. All four of these breeds, if given a chance, would work if a pup of the right sort was bought and trained properly, but if any terrierman was thinking of trying one watch out for the big ones — the over-sized terriers brought about by over-enthusiastic show breeders. Stick to the standard 10 inch terrier which you can span round the rib cage with both hands.

Scottish and Skye Terriers
But what about the Scottish Terrier I can hear some of you say, that dog bred in the north of Scotland, somewhere in the Aberdeen district, where terriermen of old used them to hunt

An early Scottish Terrier.

and kill foxes, martens, polecats and all manner of vermin. Well, again like the Norfolks and cairns and Westies it is about

10 or 11 inches at the shoulder, undocked and in three colours
– black, wheaten and brindle (an unusual colour for a terrier)
– with a long thick coat. Useless for serious earth work,
thanks to the dreaded show bench, it is now used mostly to hunt
that new quarry, the one which has taken over from the
mounted fox's mask on the wall of the hunter. It is quarry which
takes but a little tracking down and all you need is a perfectly
groomed dog and you are off on its trail. It's called a *Rosette*, a
wily creature whose pursuit has caused people to subject many a
game working breed of terrier to the atrocities of exaggeration
in build, weight, height and temperament. Yes, the rosette is
truly the working terrier's enemy.

There is a dog called the Skye Terrier, bred on the Isle of
Skye off Scotland, which is probably from the same kind of
ancestors as the Dandie Dinmont, but nevertheless the Skye
Terrier is definitely one of the oldest breeds of terriers. It
stands about 10 inches at the shoulder and is long in the body,
like a Dandie, and is steel blue in colour with silky pricked ears.
Sadly I do not know of any being used to hunt live quarry.

Dandie Dinmont

One terrier which certainly played a part in the Sealyham's
make-up is the Dandie Dinmont Terrier, an old border breed
named after one of Sir Walter Scott's characters, who owned a
pack of short-legged, long, low-to-the-ground bodied terriers.

Dandie Dinmonts of the 1890s.

The first Dandie Dinmont club was formed in 1876 and it is, without doubt, one of England's oldest terrier breeds. It has a thick, glossy and silky topknot like the Bedlington. I don't know anyone who has a Dandie Dinmont that works, although I did once see a photo of veteran working terrierman, Alf Rhodes, with his working Dandie Dinmont bitch. I like to see the old breeds being worked today.

So, which breed of terrier you choose doesn't matter as long as once it's underground, it does the job we keep them for.

Pit Bull Terriers

In the past I have been on digs where bull terriers have been present and, to be honest, sometimes the bull terrier has belonged to me, and I don't mind speaking the truth about it. They have done nothing but get in the way – all except my old dog Brock, the gentle giant on the team. American Pitbull terriers taken out on a dig would only put your terriers in even more danger than they are already.

This Staffordshire bull terrier is the exception to the rule and works well and peacefully with other terriers.

Since the American Pitbull Terrier has become popular in this country quite a few crosses have turned up, mostly crossed with lurchers, greyhounds or other bull terrier breeds. Although I have heard of pitbull-cross-Russells or pitbull-cross-lakelands, I have never seen a cross like this and I believe them to be quite useless. The pitbull is also most unsuitable to cross with a terrier. Believe me, I own pitbull terriers and they have an inborn hate for their fellow canines and cannot be trusted with other dogs at all. I would not advise anyone to purchase a pitbull-cross-terrier for earth work. Crossed with a greyhound they will produce a good lamping, or foxing lurcher, but that's all. The only way a pitbull terrier could be of any use as a working dog today is as a seizer dog at the end of a dig, and you have to ask yourself whether it is worth all the other problems to have such a dog on the team for this one purpose.

CROSSBRED TERRIERS

Some of the best terriers that I have seen working were crossbred terriers. If you do want a crossbred working terrier, I would make sure it was from working stock and use the same criteria as you would if buying a purebred one. Make sure that both parents and preferably grandparents, have worked. There is no best cross for a working terrier but my advice to anyone looking for a crossbred would be to pick either a border/lakeland or a border/Russell. These two crosses, in my mind, are as good as any other.

Border/Russell
Border/Russell is a very popular cross. The first cross is quite often black and tan or red-grizzle in colour. A few years ago I had a 10½ inch Jack Russell bitch named Meg. She was a good little worker and was the daughter of my old Jack Russell, Midge. I mated her to Toby, my border terrier dog. She had a litter of two pups, a red-grizzle dog, which I sold to my cousin, and a black and tan bitch which is my border/Russel bitch, Tess. I have bred quite a few litters of border Russells and have had a lot of success with them. I quite often get asked for a border Russell-bred dog as they are usually very easy to enter. One

47

black and tan dog pup I sold to my cousin was killing rats at five months old and at eight months while out for a walk in Cranleigh, Surrey he suddenly went to ground quite of his own accord.

Toby, the author's veteran border terrier, keeping a watchful eye on the dig.

Tess, on the right, after a ratting expedition.

Tess with her litter of border-Russell/Russell.

You can also breed a nice looking Jack Russell Terrier from a border/Russell, using a border Russell bitch and a Jack Russell dog, or vice versa. The result being some border terrier-coloured and some Jack Russell-coloured. The pups which look like the border take only the border colour and have the Jack Russell shape. The Jack Russell-coloured pups look much smarter and neater and it seems to steady the wildest strain of Russell down. The so-called pure-bred Jack Russell owners and breeders will probably call me all sorts of names now but there is no pure-bred Jack Russell, only strains of coloured terriers that breed true to type, owned by some people who breed their dogs carefully.

Lakeland/Russell

I don't know why more of the old pedigree terrier breeds do not get tried or used more often. The pure-bred pedigree show lakeland is in fact every bit as hard and vicious as its non-pedigree fell cousin. I haven't, to date, had a pedigree show-type lakeland but from what I have heard from terriermen who have trained and worked them, I think they would do the job of fox control just as well as their non-pedigree cousins. I did have a pedigree lakeland/Jack Russell once which

49

was a cracking foxing bitch and a good ratter, she had a good nose for finding vermin. I bought her from some terriermen in Portsmouth who bred her from a small leggy-type Russell bitch put to a non-working show lakeland terrier dog. When I bought her she was seven months old and hadn't done any work at all, by the time she was a year old she was finding and killing rat as a pastime, and at 13½ months old I took her out on her first foxing trip. She entered to fox almost straight away and when she was shown her fox at the end of the dig she started to bay almost immediately, with only a little encouragement. After no more than four foxing trips she had become so hard that she reduced her foxes to lifeless carcasses. I eventually sold her on as she was far too hard and we didn't have any room for an iron-hard terrier on the team, but for someone who just wanted a fox killer and didn't mind if the foxes were knocked about and the carcasses badly marked, she was ideal. The man I sold her to killed a lot of foxes with her although he didn't get much for the pelts he sold, for they were in too bad condition but, as I said to the man, the little bitch is unaware of the price of fox pelts.

Border/Patterdale

At the time of writing, I am anxiously awaiting the birth of a litter of border/patterdale pups which I have been promised a puppy from. The parents of the expected litter are two very fine workers – the border sire is out of my own border bitch Trixy, a timid and shy little bitch above ground and a noisy, brave little bitch below ground. The mother of the litter is Tony Brown's patterdale bitch, who is a fine little worker and has taken quite a few championship prizes at terrier shows up and down the country. A pup from these two dogs will be highly prized in my kennels.

Patterdale/Lakeland

One of the nicest crossbred fell-type terriers that I have seen is a patterdale/lakeland type, with a really powerful head. It is a bit too hard for me but, nevertheless, a really nice type of dog.

Russell/Patterdale

A couple of years ago I had a very old-fashioned type of patterdale bitch bred by Alan Rapley, of Rusper. She looked a little like the old Bedlington-type terrier, with long, silky topknot and silver, silky ears. I bred three litters of pups from her, two with my Russell dog, Beagle, and one with my border dog, Toby. I only saw the Russell crosses grow up and work because the border crosses seemed to be bought by people out of the district, people that I have never seen before or since. The Jack Russell/patterdales were excellent little dogs, all of them being eager to work at an early age. Some puppies turned out strangely, being smooth-coated and chocolate-coloured and even having chocolate coloured eyes. I have bred other patterdales and other patterdale-crosses but I have never bred a chocolate-coloured one since. I am not sure if it was the Jack Russell or the patterdale who threw the chocolate colouring. Although I have never seen a chocolate Jack Russell, I have seen a chocolate-coloured patterdale, which a friend of mine bought from the Lake District. It was quite funny, to look at a terrier which for years I have seen only in black or red, and see this chocolate dog with big, bright, chocolate coloured eyes.

Border/lakelands
Border/lakelands make a very good cross – I have seeen some cracking dogs of this cross working all kinds of game.

Bull crosses
To cross a pitbull with a working terrier breed would, in my mind, be ridiculous. The only advantages you would have if you had a first cross of this nature would be if you were to use it for the rat pits – killing great numbers of rats against the clock – but that's out because it's been illegal since 1911. Looking at it logically, nine out of ten pitbulls weigh-in from 40 pounds to 80 pounds, and to cross one with a working terrier, such as a Russell, lakeland, border etc, would produce a dog of about 30 pounds or possibly more. You would have to breed it from the pitbull bitch with the working terrier as sire, because most pitbull dogs are far too big to breed with any working terrier bitch. Even if you did find a small enough pitbull dog to cover your bitch, it would almost destroy a terrier bitch to pass the pups, for the heads of the pitbull pups would be far too big for a terrier bitch to pass and would probably result in a Caesarean. In my own experience of crossing smaller Staffordshire Bull

Terriers with Russells, most of the pups are dead by the time the vet does the operation, due to the bitch's constant straining and pushing. If she starts to whelp in the night and you are unaware of it, the first dead puppy could have started to go rotten and would swell up inside the bitch before you know it. This would cause infection in the womb resulting in the womb having to be removed. Thus your results for trying to breed a pitbull cross out of a terrier bitch – one Caesarean, one hysterectomy, at least half the litter of pups dead, and then, to round it off nicely, a vet's bill of well over £100. You may call me gloomy, miserable and even spoilsport but that's speaking from experience.

Pipa, a veteran rat hunting Staffordshire bull terrier.

Bull/Russell

One cross which seems to be popular is a Staffordshire Bull Terrier/Jack Russell, although the first cross is a bit too big in the chest and all sorts of problems can occur in whelping. The second cross, the Staff-Russell/Russell is a bit neater and a little less spiteful. I have seen the second cross dogs kill foxes underground as quick and as fast as the hardest northern terrier and, I might add, as silently, for most of the bull terrier bred earth dogs that I have seen have been very mute in their work underground.

Bull/Border

I once bred a litter of Staff/border pups. The bitch only reared one pup, a black and tan bitch, called Bramble who at 13 months old, I sold to a very well known terrierman. She hadn't seen any work at all but was taken on a dig and was left running loose. At the end of the dig a fox bolted and Bramble saw it running off across the downs. Bramble had never seen a fox before and wasted no time in getting to know one. She took off after it, catching it after a run across a field and holding it until help arrived. She became quite a good dog for holding and drawing fox and still is as far as I know. I have never had a cross like this since but the one that I did breed became a very useful dog indeed.

Norwich/Russell

Recently, while visiting a friend's yard, I saw a small agile little short-legged terrier bitch with a nice thick coat which was a lovely red colour. The little bitch could not keep still, searching every nook and cranny for rats and vermin. I looked at her mouth and she didn't seem as if she had seen any work to fox. I asked her owner her history and breeding and he said she had been a pet since a pup and was now 18 months old, and was given to him because she wasn't suited to indoor life. When I was told her breeding I was more than surprised, she was a Norwich Terrier/Russell. I asked if there was a price on her but her new owner was so taken by her there was no way he was going to sell, and kept her for ratting and rabbiting for which she was more than adequate. I have never owned a Norwich Terrier but if this cross was anything to go on I think any terrierman would do well to try one as a worker.

Cairn/Russell

There are so many crossbred terriers for sale today that the terrierman is somewhat spoiled for choice of a crossbred working terrier. The cairn terrier crossed with a Russell makes a very useful dog indeed. I know of one in Godalming, Surrey, which is a terrific worker and when put back to a Russell dog has produced some cracking little short-legged rough-haired Russell-type terriers which win in shows as well as work well, although some of them do have the cairns' pricked-up ears which is, in the eyes of a show ring judge, a very serious fault indeed.

Lucas Terrier

One crossbred terrier of yesteryear was the Lucas Terrier named after its creator, Sir Jocelyn Lucas of *Hunt and Working Terrier* fame. I think it was a cross between the Norfolk Terrier and the Sealyham and probably put back to the Sealyham to produce the white-bodied terrier because the first cross, Sealyham/Norfolk Terrier, would most certainly take the colour of the Norfolk Terrier, as do all first crosses. If you cross any white-bodied terrier (ie, Sealyhams, Russells and fox terriers) with a coloured terrier (ie lakeland, border, patterdale, cairn, Norfolk or Welsh Terrier) then it's almost certain that the first cross will take the colour of the latter breeds. So Lucas must have crossed his terriers a second time to produce the white-bodied dogs that you see in rare old photos of Lucas and his terriers. What a great shame it is that this old cross of terrier isn't worked or hasn't caught on through the years. Who knows, perhaps in some remote part of the country this old cross is still being bred and worked out of the reach of the show world.

Welsh/Border

One crossbred terrier I once bought from a lady in Eastbourne was a supposedly Welsh Terrier/border terrier. Although it was from a reputable breeder of borders, the lady assured me that the dog was a true first cross of the two breeds, and the only reason I doubted her words was the fact that it looked like a border/lakeland. Although it was smarter than most border/lakelands, it looked too good to be true. He was about 14 inches at the shoulder and could be spanned by a small pair of hands quite easily. He was a lovely colour of grey-blue and tan, with a good powerful jaw, and was about two years old, looked very sure of himself and hadn't seen any work before of any kind. In fact he was such a good looker that I only owned the dog for two days when I was made a very good offer for him and I am sorry to say I took it.

The man who bought him kept him for two weeks before taking him on a dig. I must confess I had visions of the dog being iron-hard but I couldn't have been more wrong. The dog had no idea of work and didn't take any interest at all in fox, rats or any other vermin. The new owner of the dog, however, took him for six more months but still the dog took no interest, not even in worrying a fox carcass. So this ideal type of terrier was left behind on foxing trips by his owner, to spend some time in the kennel, or round the house with his master's wife. The only reason the dog was kept was because his owner was also a keen showman and took, I am sorry to say, many prizes with his most useless dog, which is how it quite often goes in the show ring today. His career was in for a turn, however, as one Saturday afternoon the dog was taken along on a dig with the rest of the terriers, more for exercise than anything else, and was left running loose. A fox earth was found, holes netted and a terrier put in but the fox wasn't going to bolt and had to be dug. As they got nearer the terrier, two voices could be heard baying quite plainly. The men looked around to see if any of the other terriers had broken loose but they were all accounted for – it was the useless Welsh Terrier/border, who, suddenly at the age of 3½, finally decided to work. He must have heard the other terrier working and pushed his way past the nets and went to ground. When the diggers broke through he was right in front baying for all he was worth, and had taken quite a bit of punishment from the fox. It was no fluke or a one-off day because the next week he was to ground for eight hours, and never stopped baying once and wouldn't come out until dug to. He had finally proved himself worthy of the description – a working terrier.

That was the only Welsh Terrier cross that I have ever seen, although he was put to quite a few terrier bitches I never really heard much about his progeny, but I believe he did sire some nice looking terriers, both good and bad workers.

Border/Sealyham

The Sealyham, once a famous and well known badger digging terrier, has almost died out as a worker. Although some terriermen still keep them, I think they are in a minority. I have never seen one work but I did have the pleasure of seeing a border/Sealyham work on one occasion. It was a lovely red bitch with a rough coat and it worked fox perfectly. The bitch was going to be put to a Sealyham dog and I booked a puppy, but for some reason or other, she never whelped and I lost interest in the cross and decided to stick with the terriers I have.

Fox/Patterdale

There's a cross of terrier that I am thinking of trying – I have been toying with the idea for quite some time now but haven't had the dogs to breed them. I was thinking of buying a fox terrier bitch, a breed that I haven't had before, and putting a nice smooth-coated patterdale dog across her. The patterdale I would choose would be the smooth bull terrier-headed type. When I say bull terrier head I mean the dog with that hard, almost rhino-type skin and hard jaw muscles. I think a dog of this breeding put to a fox terrier bitch would produce a very useful dog indeed. The puppies would be patterdale coloured but put another fox terrier across the first cross and you would produce puppies of the fox terrier colour, with better jaws and more of a working instinct. Perhaps in the not too distant future I will be able to put theory into fact and give you some real information on the cross and its working potential.

Whatever your choice of a terrier, remember the reason we cross our terriers is to try and blend breeds, hoping to mix both sides' working qualities to produce the ultimate crossbred *working terrier*. Not to produce a different type of dog just for the sake of it.

—2—

Buying & bringing on a puppy

I F YOU INTEND buying a terrier pup you will want to see
its parents, that way you will get a good idea what type of
terrier your pup will turn out to be. You don't want him to
be too big, about 12–13 inches at the shoulder is about right, that
is, in my opinion, the right size for an all-round working terrier.
By that I mean a terrier which can work most earths, be they big
or small holes, and tackle any kind of reasonable sized
land-drain, and if he or she is a hard terrier, (a hard terrier
being a dog which goes in for the kill, rather than baying) then a
terrier of this stamp is quite able and is just the right size – not
too small for a fox killer and not too big and clumsy to bay and
work his quarry without getting hurt or stuck underground.

Feeding
Let us assume you have bought your terrier pup at the age of
eight to 12 weeks so your first priority is to make sure he is well
and properly fed. The first golden rule is to make any changes to
its diet slowly and the best plan is to ask the breeder for his
feeding programme and stick to this for the first few days, until
the puppy is settled, then introduce any changes to the diet
slowly. A bad attack of the runs at best will hold back your pup's
development, and at worse could be fatal.

Tiny at three and a half weeks old with Tracy, the author's wife.

Tiny at seven weeks and very active.

A typical feeding routine for a puppy of this age would be two milky porridge-type feeds and two meat feeds of something like boiled pet mince or, if you're feeling rich, Pedigree Chum for Puppies. As the weeks go by, replace the milky feeds with meat ones, increasing the quantities then reducing the number of feeds till gradually the puppy is eating the same food at the same times as an adult.

Inoculation and Worming

At the age of eight–ten weeks take your puppy to your local vet and have it inoculated before you let it out in the world. They will inoculate it against distemper, hardpad, leptospirosis, hepatitis and parvo. Parvo virus is a relatively new disease and a real killer. If people have their pups vaccinated and give adult dogs their booster jabs once a year this horrible killer disease will die down, as did distemper, which used to be widespread and a real killer, as did the other fatal diseases your pup will be inoculated against. Also worm your puppy otherwise he will have a roundworm infestation and this will severely affect his growth and development.

Training

Once your pup has been inoculated and lead trained, you can start to take him for walks and get him used to following you. Praise him for obedience, scold him for disobedience. A tennis ball is a good toy for a pup to play with – try and get him to retrieve it, he will probably try and chew it up but whatever he does with it he will be enjoying himself and that's what we want him to do, enjoy himself, doing things you want him to do.

Next get him to rag a fox brush which will really get a terrier pup's adrenaline up and make him keen to do things for you. Then if you can get hold of a large pipe about 10 foot long and about 10 inches round, roll his tennis ball through the pipe when he is chasing it. Terrier pups love all this and more. Drag the fox brush through the pipe and let him catch it halfway, but don't over do it, keep him keen for more. This way, when he sees you coming with his fox brush he will get excited, with only a little encouragement.

A young fell type ragging a dead fox.

While he is young try breaking him to ferrets. Ferrets are a good ally to a terrier, especially if it's to go ratting. Show the ferret to the pup, let the puppy smell the ferret; let the ferret be the boss and even let the ferret nip the pup just to show him who the governor is; try and get them to drink from the same bowl – do this and your terrier will develop the right kind of relationship with your ferret. My own dogs get on so well with my ferrets that lurchers, terriers and ferrets will all drink from the same bowl. Get them doing this together and hunting accidents with them will be few and far between. A terrier must also quickly learn that domestic animals are NOT fair game. Cattle, sheep, horses, pigs, goats, geese, ducks, chickens and cats (yes cats, you will not be welcome on many farms if the first thing your terrier does is kill the farm cat when you arrive to go hunting, and some farms have a great number of cats) must be out of bounds to the pup. I like to stock-break my pups at an early age, that way by the time they are young adults, domestic animals are just like part of the family to them. A game hen with a brood of chicks will soon put a terrier pup on the right side of the fence, or a grown dog for that matter.

Terriers, ferrets and lurcher all drinking milk from the same bowl. The time spent developing the right relationship in a working team will be repaid when the action gets fast and furious.

Spend as much time as possible with your pup, after all they're still only babies. If you keep your pup indoors you can be with him almost constantly and so build a good relationship with him. If you keep your puppy outside in kennels you will have to make time to spend with him. If he is outside make sure his kennel is warm, dry and draught-proof and clean. Once my pups are big enough to follow me across the fields I like to take them roughshooting. They soon get used to the sound of the gun and when they see the adult dogs getting excited when I shoot something, they really love it; especially when I shoot a squirrel. They love to worry and rag the covers with the adult terriers. Although you can have great fun roughshooting with terriers, I have only had one terrier that would retrieve fur or feather that had been shot, and that was my first border terrier Dusty. She was almost as good as a spaniel. The rest of my terriers are not so restrained, and I have a heck of a job getting anything I have shot away from them, be it fur or feather.

I like to take the pups out around the farm young, not for them to hunt or catch anything, but to look and learn from the older dogs. When they see the older dogs searching out the wood-piles, barns and ditches for rats and mice they soon want to join in the fun. By the time their milk teeth are falling out and they're getting their permanent teeth through, they're in there searching as well. Some terriers are more forward than others, some will show great keenness at work and want to start at a very early age. Some lakelands or patterdales will kill rats at five months old, while others will shy away at that tender age. The northern breeds, such as patterdale and lakelands, will try and work fox while still in puppyhood. These youngsters are best held back until their first birthday at least, a six or seven month old terrier is no match for a fullgrown fox. Some strains of terriers are famous for entering early. Terriers that enter early are not always the best workers although they are easy to start. Sometimes, the quiet, sit back types are the best and steadiest workers. I have seen some dogs entered too early, scarred up and made old before their time by being over-matched too young. My border terriers vary a lot. One bitch called Tuffy was well over three years old before she started to work properly. Her career as a working terrier has grown considerably since that day. Once a terrier is between 10–15 months old it is safe to say he is of age to start working on fox. By this time he should have killed quite a few rats, worked cover and bushes with older dogs, ragged and worried a few carcasses and be keen to do things for you.

Although terriers can be extremely good house-dogs and will guard your home and property and even be protective of their master, you don't want a spiteful dog that yaps and barks at every stranger it sees. Or a fighter. I don't like a terrier that tries to pitch a fight with every strange dog it sees. Sometimes I work my dogs with other terrier and lurchermen and no one will be keen to work their dogs with a nasty fighting terrier. Today, most terriers are a part of a small fox-hunting team consisting of two or three terriers, a couple of the right sort of lurchers and two, or maybe three men. A team like this will take a lot of foxes if operated properly and believe me, to catch foxes you have to go about it in the right way.

A young terrier eagerly awaits his turn.

—3—

Kennelling and Feeding Adult Terriers

I F YOU KEEP a number of working terriers, then it's odds on you will have to keep them in outside kennels. My own terriers are kept in kennels all year round, and are none the worse for their outside lives. A working terrier has to work in all weathers and all conditions, from a hot sunny day to bitter winter rains and frosts, sometimes being clogged with thick, wet, cold clay and dirt, so the least we can do is to feed and house them properly. Most people keep between three to six terriers but only keep two terriers kennelled in the same run, because of fights. Two terriers will fight and one will, most likely, dominate the other one but sometimes even keeping two terriers together can be disastrous. I once had a lovely little Jack Russell bitch from the late Ted Addset's strain. I kept her kennelled with Toby, my border terrier dog. They seemed to get on fine, although the little bitch got in quite a few fights with the other terriers, she and Toby got on very well together. One day Geoff and I took some of the other dogs out, leaving Toby and the little bitch in kennels together, yapping and barking at the sight of us leaving with lurchers, terriers and spades. Three hours later, on our return, we found only Toby in the run to greet us. I rushed to look in the kennel, only to find the little bitch dead, she and Toby had got into a fight and Toby won,

65

weighing 19 pounds and the little bitch 12 pounds she was no
match for him. Most terriers kennelled together soon settle
down to living in close proximity and can live like it for years.
Bull terriers must be kennelled singly and not with other dogs. A
bull terrier kennelled with any other dog is like a time bomb
waiting to go off at any second.

Make sure that you don't make your runs too small. They
want to be at least eight feet by four feet, big enough for a man to
stand up in. The covered kennel part must be big enough for
two terriers to walk in and lie down stretched out, away from
each other. Be warned – terriers can be very possessive over
their sleeping beds. A box of four feet by three feet six inches is
about right for two terriers. Keep your terriers' house clean and
dry. If you put asphalt on the roofs and use felt nails, cover each
nail with a waterproof solution, like rubberoid Mastick, as this
will stop rain from getting into the kennel. All wooden surfaces
should be treated with creosote to prevent the wood from
rotting. Sheep dip mixed in with Creosote will help to kill any
mange mites that get into your wood. While I am on the subject,
all working terriers come into contact with mange through
working foxes, some of which are riddled with it. There are so
many cures I can't go into them all, and often they are useless
anyway, so I shall only mention one of them and that's the best
one: Coopers Lice and Mange Liquid is a sheep dip that costs
£16–£18 a gallon tin. Mixed up in a large household bath, dogs
with the worst dose of mange can be cured. It has all the
directions on the tin for mixing with water. It is also the best
thing I've found for killing fleas, ticks and just about everything
your dog can get in his coat and skin. I mix a fresh tub up at the
beginning of each summer and keep topping it up as I go
through the year. Any infected dog is dipped daily until cured.

Back to the dog run and kennels; if your runs are on grass or
dirt, or some other non-solid surface, I would advise you to put
down some concrete or some paving slabs, laid on sand.
Old-fashioned concrete is the best – durable, washable and it
looks good. Washed with a little Jeyes Fluid, germs will be kept at
bay, and in this day and age we need all the help we can at
keeping disease and germs down to a minimum. When a terrier
has taken a lot of punishment at his work and needs a few weeks
in sick bay, it's a good idea to get a heat lamp rigged up,

A Jack Russell, her nose swelling rapidly after a tangle with a fox.

especially if they're living outside in winter months. Don't get the infra-red light, get the white one, it gives out a hot, white light like an ordinary light bulb and is much more suitable than the red light. A terrier kept outside after taking a lot of bad punishment will need one, for a few days, to keep the chill off him.

Wounds

For wounds there are all sorts of different remedies. For fox bites, I clean all wounds with a piece of cotton wool dipped in Dettol water. Bad rips need stitching. If they need stitching or have a puncture wound they get a long-lasting penicillin injection, which helps reduce swelling as well as dealing with any infection. I have found fox bites to be very poisonous, probably because the fox eats some very 'high' food. To be quite honest though, it doesn't matter what kind of bite or cut your terrier gets, treat them all with the same caution and delicacy and keep them clean. You will enjoy your dog's good health every time you work him so please look after your working terriers.

Terriers will work their hearts out for you, going deep into the dark, damp ground looking for their quarry, and they will stay there for as long as it takes; regardless of self-sacrifice. So the least we can do for them is to keep them warm, dry and clean and tend to their wounds properly. Keep them in good health and help them to live to a ripe old age, in as much comfort as possible. Surely they deserve it.

Feeding the Working Terrier

There's no best or worst food for a working terrier. Different dogs and puppies prefer different foods. Possibly the most popular foods are the ones where you add boiling water or gravy of some sort, like Vitalin, Wilsons, Valumix or the other kinds which have a little more meat added to the mix, such as Olympic Gold, Silver and Bronze. In my mind Purena is the best one but certainly the most expensive of the sack foods. It is ideal for conditioning dogs and getting them fit, for it has more protein and less fat content than any other foods. Then there's the tinned foods which can work out a little bit expensive if you keep a lot of dogs. If you only have two or three dogs, tinned food such as Pal or Chunky, mixed with some biscuits such as Winalot, will suffice quite well. Butcher's scraps, the scraps of off-cut meat from your local butcher, is ideal if boiled up and fed when it is a little warm. I don't like to keep my dogs on the same food for a great length of time and vary their diet from time to time. I like to see my dogs keen and eager for food and having good, healthy appetites. One food I found to be very good, and my dogs certainly enjoyed it and didn't get sick of eating it, was chicken and turkey offal, or should I say, chicken and turkey bodies. I had a meat-offal contract from North Farm, Findon, near Worthing at 5p per pound. Needless to say the turnover of the meat factory must have been enormous, I was one of seven meat contractors taking as much as three hundred pounds of chicken and turkey away each day. My dogs thrived on it boiled or raw. Even the turkey and chicken heads, once boiled and left overnight to go cold and set in their own jelly, looking a little like a cannibal's jellied eels, were loved by my terriers, lurchers, and even ferrets. Although my dogs thrived on this diet, I must add that every so often I bought a bag of dog food to give them a change now and again. Since the North Farm estate and poultry units at Findon went bankrupt my glorious food supply dried up, more's the pity for I fear I will never find another food supply as plentiful and as cheap as this one. Another good food supply is your local slaughter house. Sheep, cattle and pigs' heads can be bought for as little as 5p each. I don't bother to skin or clean animal heads, I simply feed them either raw or boiled and dogs love them, although I wouldn't expect puppies to eat such foods. I will only feed hard, wholefood like this to dogs of six months or over. Young puppies need clean and easy food that does not need to be pulled apart and ripped to pieces. Rabbits are a good food. I boil them whole for my dogs, only taking out the rabbits' guts. Sometimes I even leave the skins on as well. Adult working terriers can cope quite well with all this kind of food and do very well on it, despite what the show-bench people would have you think.

Feeding the Working Terrier Bitch and Puppies
The most important thing in a puppy's life is that it's given a good enough start in life, and by that I mean given the right food and drink and wormed properly. To do this you must start even before the puppies are born. When the dam of the pups is six or seven weeks pregnant she should be wormed out thoroughly, with round and tapewormers, and again when the pups are born. A nursing bitch needs double the food and milk whilst rearing her pups, because, you must remember, you are not feeding one dog anymore, but several. My terrier bitch Tess always has between six and nine pups and the appetite of any lurcher or greyhound and she bloats herself out with milk until she looks like a hairy four-legged toad.

Once the puppies are about 3½ weeks old it's a good idea to try them with a little milky Ready Brek. They probably won't lap it up by themselves immediately and will need a little help to learn to lap and drink from a bowl. You can teach them this quite easily, just by dipping their noses in the bowl of milky Ready Brek or porridge. They will soon get the knack of it and be lapping and drinking in no time at all. Judging by my own

69

puppies, they will also walk through and sit in the bowl of food, and generally get more food on themselves than they do inside them.

Once they are eating milky foods, at around four weeks, they will want four feeds a day: A milky porridge feed for breakfast, soft, meaty food such as Pedigree Chum, Chunky or Pal, or a little boiled pet mince is ideal at lunch time. In the afternoon some more milky foods, just some ordinary cow's milk will do quite nicely, and in the evenings, another porridge feed. As the puppies get to five or six weeks, they should be having two meat feeds a day. Dispense with one of the milky feeds and supplement it with the meat feed. Keep up this feeding until they're eight weeks old, then move them onto one porridge feed, two milk feeds and two meat feeds a day, and your puppies should thrive and grow quite nicely.

At the age of 10 weeks I like to wean my puppies. Some breeders say it's best to take your pups away from their dams at around eight weeks, but at eight weeks some puppies look, and act, a little too much like five or six week old pups. I always leave my pups on their dams until they're 10 weeks old. I would also like to say that some eight week old pups look a little bit older than eight weeks old, in fact some look like 12 week old pups but even with these big, bouncy pups it will not hurt to leave them on their dams for the extra two weeks. Your terrier bitch will not suffer from this extra feeding provided you look after her while she's nursing her puppies, giving her lots of milk whenever she wants it, food as well. As I have said before a terrier bitch, with pups, will eat twice as much as normal while fetching up a litter of pups.

Another thing to remember is that when a bitch has had a litter of pups, it takes a lot of the calcium and glucose out of her body, so a lot needs replacing. When you give your bitch her milk, put two eggs in the bowl and mix them in well. Glucose powder in the water bowls is also a good idea. A couple of eggs a day is as good to a bitch as any conditioning tablets that you can buy in a packet. Another idea for a whelping bitch, is when you make your first pot of tea in the mornings, if you leave any, don't tip it wastefully down the sink, tip it in your terriers' bowl with just a little milk. My terriers all love a morning cuppa when the opportunity arises – not only the bitches with pups. Another milk you can get is calf milk. You can buy half hundredweight bags, which is ideal if you keep a lot of dogs. A bag of this powdered milk lasts forever it seems. It can be bought from any animal feed shop. I believe it's about £15 a bag now, but for the time it lasts it's really quite cheap, and dogs and puppies which are given it seem to thrive and do better on it than with any other milk supplement. If you don't have many dogs Lactol from your local pet shop is probably your best bet.

If you have a terrier bitch with pups and you are worried that something is wrong don't wait to see what happens; phone the vet immediately and describe the symptoms and if necessary get him out to see the bitch. I know it's expensive but if your bitch does go down with something like milk fever you don't have much time to do something about it before she dies.

A patterdale type emerges from an earth.

—4—

How Not to Get Arrested

THE LAWS CONCERNING badger digging have been progressively tightened over the years. It all started with the Badgers Act in 1973 which was amended by the Wildlife and Countryside Act 1981 and the Wildlife and Countryside (Amendment) Act 1985. The last Act made it an offence to dig for badgers under any circumstance, whether or not you have permission from the landowner and it states that the terrierman has to prove that he was not digging for badgers. If you think about it that is not very easy, even if you were digging for a fox in a sett that you knew to have been abandoned by badgers. This must be about the only law in this country where you are guilty until proved innocent. There is a BFSS publication *'The Five Rules for the Terrierman'* which you might find helpful to have on the shelf to make sure you stay on the right side of the law. But the simple fact is that digging badgers these days is not worth the fine, or even prison sentence. If you get caught digging a badger sett, occupied or unoccupied by badger, you are going to find·it virtually impossible to prove your innocence in a court of law.

Now, thanks to the League Against Cruel Sports, or as most of us know them as the anti-hunt supporters, when a badger is being a nuisance to a farmer, and believe me they can do some damage when they want to, the farmer can no longer ask a terrierman to come in and move them (alive) because they'll face a fine of up to £2,000, or even a prison sentence. So the farmer has to call in the Ministry of Agriculture and the government official has to see what damage has been done, and whether or not the brock is a pest or not and if he is, and the farmer definitely wants him moved, then the worst happens. I think by now you have already guessed it, the badger is gassed and killed without being given one chance of escape. The officials from the Ministry of Agriculture and the government assure us it's quite painless, perhaps they've tried it on someone – another government official, hopefully – but I don't think so!

I am not going to be so naïve as to say that there's no cruelty involved in hunting. In hunting there is the aspect of death and no matter which way you dispatch your quarry, if it has to be killed, there's no good way to take a life. The best is the quickest and most painless way which is as often as not a gun. At least with hunting a fox, a badger or even a rat or rabbit has more than an even chance to get away and live another day. To put it another way – would you, if you were a fox or badger, rather pit your wits and cunning against a terrier or lurcher and its owner, somewhere that you know all the escape routes, all the back entrances and secret places to hide, or be asleep in an earth to find all entrances and exits blocked and suffocate to death on a deadly gas, or pass through some gap in a hedge, some old run through a fence, to find a snare around your neck?

To be fair, if set properly, a snare can catch a fox in full flight and break its neck causing it to die almost immediately. I have tried snaring and to be quite truthful I set somewhere in the region of 30 snares and I think I caught three or maybe four foxes, all of which were very much dead when I found them. The law states that you can snare foxes, rabbits and even rats as they come under the same heading: *VERMIN*. You cannot snare on public footpaths, bridleways, parks or even allotments, definitely not on roadsides, public lanes or railway lines. All these places are out. I would like to point out that if you do set snares, check them night and morning; once a day or once every other day isn't good enough. Not only the so-called vermin use the runs and hedgerow passes, so do domestic animals such as cats and dogs and you definitely don't want those in your snares.

74

A vixen caught by a snare. Had she been accounted for by a terrierman and humanely killed, her suffering would have been a lot less.

Most snares today are fitted with a stopper, stopping the snare from closing on smaller animals, such as cats and small dogs. The idea is that a dog would be used to being restrained by a lead or rope, so once it put its head through the snare it would realise it was caught and sit down until the snare is checked and the dog released and set free, unharmed.

75

It makes me laugh sometimes because so many times I have been either rabbiting, fox digging, hare coursing, ferreting or shooting and someone has informed the authorities and either a police officer or RSPCA man has come to interfere and find out our intentions. If someone comes along when we are ratting they don't bother us, even on the rare occasion when asked what we were doing and replied 'rat killing'. Their answer has been 'yuk, I hate those horrid creatures'.

Now that the badger is, without doubt, not the legitimate quarry of the terrierman the rat, fox and rabbit are now under much more pressure than they have been for years. It seems now that rats and rabbits are on the increase, and so are the fines if caught poaching them. So wherever you go to work your dogs make sure you have permission and remember no matter how desolate the piece of land it belongs to someone and there is no quicker way of flushing out an owner than to start poaching his land. Ask any farmer about rats, rabbits, foxes and even the supposedly harmless badgers and he will state, without hesitation, they are pesty vermin to be given no mercy, but venture out on the same farmer's land to do some ferreting and you will be branded as a no good lazy poacher. Ask if you can control the pests on his land and the most popular answer is 'sorry, let it to a shoot', whether it's true or not. But, as in all things, you can find some farmers who will be happy for you to rid them of pests. If you are friendly with any gamekeepers you can quite often get some good land to work your terriers on. Most keepers are only too pleased for you to rid the land of foxes and you will have all the legal permission you want.

When I was a boy you could walk down the road with lurchers, terriers and ferrets and hardly anyone would take any notice of you. You could walk any wasteland or common land with terriers, spades or ferrets with very little, or no, harassment at all. Not any more. Try and walk down a country lane or road with terriers and spades and you will be branded a 'badger digger' or as I saw printed in the local press recently, a badger baiter.

How easy it is now to get arrested for badger digging: all you have to do is enter your terrier in a sett the badgers have left and has been taken over by foxes. Your terrier starts baying his fox and you start digging to the sound of your dog. Whilst you are digging some busybody with nothing better to do comes along, walking his or her pet dog, and sees a horrible man with a large looking spade and a spiteful looking dog, who's digging up the badger sett, to kill the badgers in there; or at least that's what gets reported to the police. Then, along comes the police with the good citizen, who points out that there's lots of baby badgers in there, as well as the full grown ones, which don't hurt anyone. Now try to explain to the police, who don't know what they're doing anyway, that you're not digging badgers and that you are foxhunting and, foxes being classed as vermin, it is perfectly legal to take them with the use of terriers, nets and spades. You will be fighting a losing battle. You can say 'Let me dig it out and show you there's only a fox in here', but they won't let you. If your terrier comes out for a breather and has a few nips on his muzzle, then you have had it. Try and get out of that one without a heavy fine, or even a few weeks or months at Her Majesty's pleasure.

This badger sett is definitely in use. The small tree shows the tell tale signs of being used as a scratching post.

The fact that you know there is a fox and not a badger down there is very different to being able to prove it in a court of law. So stick to fox earths where you can be sure of only finding fox and there is no evidence of past occupation by badger. Before you enter your terrier look around for signs of discarded bedding, a tree being used as a scratching post, badger hairs around the entrance – all warning signs that brock could be at home. Having said this it is possible for a badger to have just moved into a fox earth and their being no tell tale signs, unfortunately the law makes no allowance for this.

Since the 1985 Act was passed quite a few people have been caught and prosecutions have been brought against them for digging and killing badgers. Badgers can be poached, but is it worth it? The hides are worthless. On the whole a badger carcass is worthless, unlike fox pelts – around December you can get as much as £20 each for these.

Some antis go as far as staking out a well-known terrierman's home and following him when he goes to work his terriers, hoping to catch him in the act of illegal badger digging. Some even go as far as staking out the badgers' setts themselves, hoping to catch a team of badger diggers in the act, so to speak.

—5—

Entering a Terrier to Fox

THE EASIEST WAY to enter a terrier to fox is by taking him out on digs and tieing him up near the earth so he can hear the adult terrier baying at its fox. When you dig down to the adult terrier the fox should be a few feet away. If so take the unentered dog and let him see the terrier baying his fox, if the pipe is big enough let the youngster join the adult and see if he will bay as well. This way he'll get up his confidence. Let this go on for a while and then quietly take away the adult dog so he will be in there doing it himself. After a while take him out, humanely kill the fox and then let the young dog join in ragging the carcass with the other terriers. This is to reward their efforts. I have heard people say their dogs don't worry a carcass but, believe me, all the working terriers I have seen will rag a carcass.

Next time you take the young dog out let him loose with the adult terrier. Let him follow the other terrier to ground if the fox earth is not too deep. If it is, don't enter your young dog. Find a small earth for him so they can either bolt the fox or bottle him up quickly as a young terrier needs lots of early successes to give him confidence at his job. When you work your dogs don't stomp your way up to the earth loudly, encouraging your dog to go down the main entrance – by doing this you telegraph your presence to Mr Fox. Instead, take your time, size up the earth

Two terriers owned by Alan and David Wilkinson watch and listen while another terrier works an earth.

and let your dogs find their own entrance – after all they're the ones that have to find the fox. Position a couple of lurchers properly, be very quiet and still, and your terrier will disappear to ground, find his fox and, if the fox doesn't know you are out there, he should bolt and be taken by the lurchers. Some foxes, when hearing a terrier enter the earth, will sit just inside the earth, almost waiting for a terrier to give them that little push from behind. If he sees a man walking around looking in each hole he will not bolt and that's why foxing should be like a military operation. Some people may laugh at this but if you want to catch foxes that's how it's got to be. I remember once when waiting for a fox to bolt in an old badger sett in Storrington. The badgers had left the sett and a pair of foxes had taken it over. One fox had bolted into the net but Tess, my border/Russell bitch, had trouble bolting the remaining fox. I went to listen at one of the holes and came face to face with a fox that promptly disappeared back down into the sett. It took Tess two hours to bolt him, and all because I looked into the hole.

The author's lurcher watching and waiting.

If you do let your young terrier go to ground with an experienced dog make sure it's a terrier that won't bite or tackle the youngster below ground. Make sure it's a dog that will let the young terrier have a go, letting him come forward and bay face to face with his fox. I have used this method of entering a great number of times, with a lot of success. So many young dogs have

been spoiled by another dog pushing and biting from behind. I
once bought a nice looking Jack Russell bitch, 12 months old,
that had been to ground twice to fox. I kept her for a full week
and she settled down straight away, getting very attached to me.
On the seventh day we took her on a foxing trip. She worked
cover like a dream with the other terriers. We came to our first
fox earth along a hedge and I let loose my border bitch Lady and
the new bitch. Lady disappeared and began to bay immediately.
The new bitch ran around each and every hole getting very
excited, going in up to her tail and rushing back out. We tied her
up and the fox finally bolted and was taken by the lurchers
Blondy and Whippy. The new bitch joined in ragging the
carcass as if she had bolted it herself. We tried five or six more
earths that day but she wasn't interested in going to ground. A
few days later I found out she had been entered to ground and
was working very well when one day her mother was entered
behind her and, in a frenzy to get to the fox, chewed at the little
bitch's behind and pushed her into the fox. The experience was
so bad she was terrified of going to ground, to have it happen
again. I tried her for six more months but she would not have
anything to do with earth work, although she killed rats as
quickly as any of my other terriers. I sold her to a ratcatcher
friend of mine who still has her to this day. She has become quite
famous in her district as a ratter (and not as an earth dog). So,
that's what happens when a young terrier gets used wrongly – it
quite often gets ruined for life.

Once your terrier is going to ground on his own you can run
him through some small earths. Don't enter him in too big a
place too early in his career as a working terrier or he might have
trouble making contact with his fox and, as I've said before, a
young terrier needs early success and encouragement to give
him confidence to do his job properly. Beagle, my Jack
Russell-type terrier, named for his voice and colour, was the
easiest terrier to enter that we have ever had. At 13 months old, I
walked up to a fox earth with him running loose. Geoff was
nearby with Blondy the lurcher. He ran around each hole and
then went back to the first and disappeared down it. Almost
immediately he started to bay and chased his fox underground.
A minute or two later a bright red fox bolted. Geoff slipped
Blondy the lurcher behind him but the fox had a bit too much

cover to hide in and after a small run disappeared into the woods and was long gone. Beagle came out with only a nip on his nose and cheek – that was Beagle's first foxing trip.

Border terriers ragging a dead fox.

That afternoon we entered Lady. It wasn't a deep earth but it covered a very wide area and I could hear Lady baying and moving her foxes around. One fox suddenly bolted and Geoff slipped Blondy and Whippy, the two lurchers, and they took their fox with very little effort or fuss. The other fox was not so keen to leave his home. Lady seemed to run him from one end of the earth to the other, she was popping out of one hole and diving into another. When Lady came out again we let Beagle go in with her. It was a chance for Beagle to learn something from her and for Lady to get some help from him. After Lady and Beagle chased the fox around for something like 15 minutes, he decided to leave his home and bolted from a hole I had placed a net over. He almost kicked his way free and Geoff slipped

Blondy on him. The fox and Blondy became locked jaw to jaw – a painful situation. Geoff despatched the fox and let the dogs rag the carcasses. Beagle went from strength to strength after that day and he is probably one of the best terriers that I have at the moment.

Terriers enter differently, some dogs start early, some dogs start late: I bought a border terrier once that was three years old and had never seen work of any kind. She entered to fox straight away and worked for the next five years until she was retired. My brother Robert bred a litter of Jack Russell pups and sold one of them to a pet home; three years later he bought her back. She hadn't been worked at all. She is a lovely little bitch, her sire is my Jack Russell dog, Beagle, and her mother a little border/Russell who throws Russell-type pups. We took her out on a foxing trip and she was running loose with Beagle and the two lurchers. They were about 30 yards in front of us hunting up a part of a wood that I don't know very well. We reached the end of the wood and the two terriers were not in sight. Blondy and her young son Flash were taking a lot of interest in a stretch of hedgerow and when I got there I found it was a small earth. I could hear a dog baying and I thought it was Beagle but my brother caught up and Beagle was following him. It was the little Russell bitch. She had gone to ground and was obviously baying at her fox. She had't worked before and this area didn't have any known earths in it, but by leaving her and the lurchers loose they had found this earth. Robert went back to the track to fetch two spades and with a little help from Beagle we soon got the little bitch and her fox out with not too much fuss. That was her first trip out with working dogs and now she is a very clever little worker. This doesn't mean that any adult terriers will work, remember the working bloodlines are very strong in the little terriers I have mentioned.

I have had terriers of all breeds that have been useless. I once had a cairn terrier that would kill rats as fast as any other terrier and was one of the best bushing terriers on rabbits I have seen, and would happily rag a fox carcass for hours. She would not go to ground and wasn't interested in any earth or dig but show her a rat and she was off. I have a Staffordshire Bull Terrier that's on the small side and will go to ground if the earth is big enough. She is as good as any other terrier at working cover, kills rats

A young border terrier with one of his first foxes.

with other terriers and doesn't fight or pick on them. She can also smell out rats or rabbits wherever they are and kill them with a crushing bite. I call her Brock and she lives up to her namesake – quiet and gentle until provoked. I have some other bull terriers but none of them will mix and join in with the other terriers like Brock will, she must have a love for hunting. Not all Staffs are as biddable as my old brock is. Some will pick on the first dog they see and will not take any interest in killing rats or doing anything else but fight, and you do not want that in a terrier team. A team is what you and your terriers must be, with you at the head of it, deciding where to enter your terrier. Decide what earth you will work and let him decide which part of the earth he wants to try first.

Listening for the terrier baying below ground.

I don't use fox nets much, the only time I use them on earths is if they cover a wide area, then you can cover one side with two running dogs. When I work my terriers in drains I always use a net. A lot of foxes can be taken from drains. A net over one end, a terrier quietly put in the other and in a few minutes your net should be loaded. Check the drains before you work them, make sure they're not linked up to a network of drains running for miles under the countryside. These vast complexes are death-traps to a terrier but the straight-through land drains hold a great number of foxes. One drain at the top of my road almost always has a fox in it. Another drain I know has foxes which rear litter after litter of cubs in there year after year; using them like they were old breeding earths. Generation after generation, I believe, foxes to use the same earths, runs and feeding grounds. Some foxes refuse to leave a drain, or cannot leave for some reason or another, such as one end being blocked up, and that's when a terrier that will draw a fox is priceless. A collar and a long line attached to it is a good thing, especially if the collar is a terrier locator.

Possibly the easiest place to catch a fox is artificial earths like the ones put down by fox-hunts, sporting farmers or keepers. There's one I know of that's made out of an old 45 gallon oil-drum and a 12 foot long and 10 inch round land drain. Foxes are taken from this earth so easily that if there's only one fox there all you need is a net and a stick. Most artificials are made out of old railway sleepers and put in parts of the countryside where foxes can rear cubs in peace without harassment from man and beast, or should I say man and terrier? Don't get carried away with the idea that every time you take your terriers out you will catch great numbers of foxes, because you won't. Some days you won't even see a sign of a fox, every earth, drain or cover will draw blank. You will probably wonder what's wrong with you or your dogs but nothing will be wrong, you will just be having one of those days that we all have, if we only like to admit it. Sometimes I have gone out two days running and the only thing I have caught is a cold.

There is one day I shall never forget. We had been asked to move a fox from a farm to a place 10 miles away and we had been digging quite some time and had reached a depth of five feet. The ground was hard going through thick, soggy clay and I could hear the terrier baying his fox. Suddenly at five feet we broke through. We opened up the hole to take the fox and found it was about four feet up the pipe and the little terrier was holding him very well. I took the terrier out so Geoff could catch the fox. There was a side-pipe that came out at the place the terrier had been baying, but I was unaware of this and through my ignorance the fox make his getaway back into the larger and much deeper part of the earth. By this time night had all but fallen and Reynard was given best. It's at times like this that I say angrily 'no more of this for me, digging my guts out in all weathers just for the sake of it'. When I calm down and stop blaming everyone from the local traffic warden to Margaret Thatcher and own up to it being my fault, the worst day out doesn't seem too bad. Believe me you can learn something new everytime you go out with your dogs. Looking back, even on the disaster trips where dogs' lives have been lost, they don't seem as bad as they did at the time it happened.

One occasion always comes to mind when we work the earths in one particular place. It's a wooded bank about 600 yards long with earths scattered all the way along it. At one end there's a deep and very old badger sett. On the day I remember we tried a

A fox drive on a small estate using terriers and guns.

three hole fox earth that didn't look dangerous and we had bolted foxes from it before with no trouble. This time it looked quite good. I let loose Tammy, a little patterdale bitch and she disappeared to ground. After a minute or two she made contact with her fox, then an hour passed and we could not get an exact mark on her, so we entered Tess to find her. Tess has a very good voice, and could soon be heard baying. It sounded to be coming more from one of the holes than up through the ground, so we decided to follow the pipe. It didn't sound deep but we dug five feet into the bank and they seemed to be just a few feet further on but the pipe was getting very narrow. By nightfall we had dug in a great depth and Tess had stopped baying, so help was sent for. Doug Cooper arrived on the scene. After several hours more digging a very tired and cramped Tess was pulled out. The pipe was so narrow it was amazing she got down there. Tess was taken to a nearby vet for some first class attention. Next Doug pulled out a vixen which had been dead for quite some time and then Tammy who was dead. The pipe was so narrow and air was very short, suffocation had killed her.

If I hadn't entered Tess this horrible experience might not have happened. I would like to say that if I had had a terrier locator I would have reached the dogs a lot sooner and saved the life of a brave and courageous little terrier. The earth was very deceptive – it looked like a small, shallow three hole fox earth but underground it was a series of deep narrow tunnels. We did not have a locator then but now we don't go without one. I would like to advise any terrierman who does not own a locator to purchase one straight away. They save a lot of walking around in circles and lying down with your ear flat to the ground. Some terriermen say they're only for boys and your dog will get itself caught up in roots but all this is rubbish. I have used them in every kind of earth there is and none of my dogs have come to any harm. Every time your terrier goes to ground he is in danger, that's part and parcel of a terrier's job. Don't listen to the man who says 'I've had dogs all my life, I know everything there is to know about working terriers'. Nobody knows it all. You can work terriers for 50 years and still learn something new every day. I know some people who have had dogs all their lives and don't know anything about them and I also know men who have had dogs for a short time and have learned a great deal.

Recently I went to a local terrier and lurcher show. It was an enjoyable day out for all the family. We made new friends and met old ones. One man was talking to a gang of young lads standing next to us and I overheard part of their conversation. The man, who would have looked more at home in a hippy

A Jack Russell has difficulty getting out of a bolt hole.

commune than at a terrier show, boasted that he had been badger digging and baiting since he was ten-years-old and of how many badgers he had caught in the last 12 months, and was holding forth on what kind of dog is best for fox and badger killing. I looked at him and his podgy little brown dog that was far too fat and round and didn't look one bit like a working terrier. The young lads were taking in every word he said as the gospel truth. It's men like this that give the wrong impression to youngsters and the general public. Men who have never worked a dog, or trained one, in their lives and are just as keen to brag about the sport wrongly to anti-fieldsport officials as to young lads at a terrier show. People like this are parasites on the back of any fieldsport and should be totally ignored. I don't like the idea of badger baiting, it's nothing to do with terrier work and terriers have nothing to do with it. Badger baiting was a cruel sport of the last century, involving a badger being put in a box and a bull terrier-type dog encouraged to pull him out. The winner was whichever dog could pull the badger out in the fastest time. So please don't get the sport of fox and the now illegal badger digging mixed up with this cruel, inhuman, murderous pastime of Old England. The fox is still legitimate quarry now but digging and taking badgers alive and unharmed with terriers is still the best way of moving them in my mind and it seems a pity that under the present legislation where it is illegal to dig a badger the only option is to call in the ministry and have it killed if it is causing a nuisance rather than moving it someplace where it will be doing no harm to anyone.

A terrier cannot hurt a badger in anyway what-so-ever and if a terrier does mix it with a badger it's the terrier that comes off worst and not the badger. It is impossible for a terrier to kill a badger, or to harm him in any way, so disregard all those stories of men owning badger-killing dogs because that's what they are, simply stories. An adult terrier, weighing about 16 pounds and with a fairly good jaw, can kill a fox without much trouble; not many foxes are much heavier than an average terrier. But if a terrier tries to kill a badger it's a different story. The average badger weighs between 25 or 30 pounds but there are much heavier ones about. A badger will stratch with his long and sharp front claws as well as use his large canine teeth. A badger will soon put a terrier out of action for good, doing most of the damage under his jaw, on his nose and down the front of a dog's chest, neck and legs.

Some terriers prefer working badger to fox. Some years ago a border terrier bitch of mine, entered to badgers in her second year. We were asked by a pig farmer friend to move a badger that was to go to another farm where it couldn't be a nuisance. We arrived at the sett which looked quite small with only a small amount of old bedding grass spread about the entrance. A Jack Russell dog was entered and he began to bay almost straight away. After chasing the badger around for a few minutes he settled down and with a bit of listening we got a steady mark on

91

him. He was four feet down and the digging was quite good. The two borders were tied up nearby and one was getting on our nerves with her non-stop barking and yapping. I let her loose for a minute and, as if she had done it all her life, she just slipped to ground. I was very surprised. She had been on a lot of digs and had been loose many times and hadn't gone to ground before. This was the day she was finally ready to start work and

Terriers are an invaluable asset to the fell hounds. Here the North Pennine on the fells above Alston.

start she certainly did. It took her a couple of minutes to find the Jack Russell when she did she began giving short, sharp yaps. She kept it up and when we broke through she was right there at the front, finally proving herself. That was her first day as a working terrier and her career as a worker grew considerably from that time. Sometimes, on a long dig she'd stay a full day, refusing to quit even when called – she would not leave her quarry. She would not win any show but if rosettes were given for courage, gameness and working ability, I think

Tony Brown's Lakeland dog with a fox which would not bolt.

she would be placed every time. Personally, I like a terrier with good looks as well as being able to work but if he is as ugly as an old boot and does the job we ask of him, then he will be placed above any good looking non-worker in my esteem.

Some terriers will start working fox and kill them with great keenness and all you can hear above gound is the noise of the fight. I had a border terrier dog who would kill foxes if they didn't bolt and on one occasion, while out foxing some years ago came across badgers by accident and he was lucky to come out of the fight alive. One day we were working some earths at Thakeham, not far from where I live. It was a large earth on a sandstone bank and when I checked it over it smelt very strongly of foxes. As it was late February and it was well trodden with fox footprints we all decided it was definitely foxes in the earth, so the border terrier was entered. He is not a fast worker and it took him a long time to find his quarry. We stood both sides of the earth with the lurchers trembling with excitement, waiting for a flash of red to come flying out of the ground. Then we heard the dog make contact with his fox. We were waiting for a fox to bolt but nothing did. We let the lurchers go and after a minute or two the dog came out with the whole of his bottom jaw mutilated and two bad holes in his chest. I literally had to dive on him before he went to ground again. It was definitely no fox that had made these wounds and he was bleeding very badly. He had come across a badger and tried to deal with the badger as he would a fox, and came off much the worse for his efforts. There was no sign of a badger living in the earth and it smelt so strongly of fox that if it hadn't been for his scars I wouldn't have thought there was a badger in there at all. We ran a little Russell bitch that was steady to badgers through the earth and she didn't make contact with any foxes. So there must have only been the badger at home. I expect that when the badger moved in the foxes moved out leaving a nice booby trap for our terrier. This story is worth remembering because under the law as it now is you could be arrested for badger digging when you didn't even know there was one there until it was too late.

Don't get carried away with the idea that a fox cannot really hurt a terrier because it can. I have seen terriers' heads swollen out of all proportion due to infection from foxbites. I once had a patterdale bitch that had her eye bitten so badly by a fox that she lost it completely through infection. The fox's bite is not like the bite or rakes of the badger. The fox tends to leave his marks on the top of the dog's muzzle and cheeks, not so much making punctures like a badger bite, but more of a slashing bite. I have even seen terriers' jaws broken after jaw to jaw confrontations with foxes. Nevertheless, I have terriers with small jaws that can kill foxes but I always think a small dog with a big heart is better than a big dog with a small heart.

Deno, Slim Farmer's border terrier, an excellent fox drawing dog.

Slim Farmer, ex-hunt terrierman and now a gamekeeper, has a nice pair of small border terrier bitches which are marvellous workers to fox. They have spent most of their working life in hunt service, working for hunts from Suffolk to Devon, and have spent quite a while at the Crawley and Horsham in my area. Slim also has a border terrier dog called Deno who is practically a legend in his own time, almost mastering the art of drawing foxes from drains in one day's hunting with the Crawley and Horsham: Hounds were hunting in a large wood for quite some time and finally marked at a land drain and Deno was entered to either bolt or draw his fox. Deno made contact with his fox and drew it from the drain without much fuss, and went back down the drain again. There was another fox in there, which Deno also dragged out. After drawing his second fox he went back

95

again down the drain and dragged out a third fox. One at a time Deno dragged out seven foxes – surely a record.

A good friend of mine, Tony Brown from Crawley, a very accomplished terrierman, is of the same opinion as myself about working lakeland terriers – that they are best worked single-handed and that they do not need any help from other terriers. If any help is given they will sometimes viciously reject it. Tony works border terriers as well as patterdales and lakelands and has found that his borders entered as early and as quickly as his lakelands did. Tony has a nice looking border dog which is a really good worker as well as having won many shows. He has been working since he was eight months old and is a real stayer, refusing to leave his quarry once he has found it, and he will work well with other terriers. The pure bred lakeland terrier has a much harder disposition and, although we have worked more than one patterdale together, we would not work more than one lakeland terrier at the same time. I once saw two lakelands entered together in a small fox earth. After a minute or two one dog came out and quickly disappeared down another hole. What happened next was quite a mystery at first. A great fight broke out under the ground – as one dog went in, another was coming out and both dogs met head on. Neither dog would give the other one an inch of ground and they locked onto each other. Luckily they were only a short distance under the ground and were reached very quickly. It was quite funny afterwards but it wasn't very funny to the owner of the two dogs, who solved his problem his own way – by advertising one of them in *Exchange and Mart*. The easiest way to have solved the problem in my opinion, would have been to work them and kennel them singly. The patterdale terrier, on the other hand, if you get hold of the right strain, is quite a biddable dog.

Please always look after the earths you work. If you dig them don't leave them looking like bomb sites with big holes all over the place. It doesn't do an earth any harm to be dug, as long as you fill back the holes and leave the ground as tidy as you found it. I have gone to work earths with my terriers and arrived to find holes big enough for a full-grown cow to fit into, so please spend the extra 10 minutes and look after the land and sport. Another thing is that not many landowners will welcome you with your terrier and spade if you abuse his land. It's up to you and me, and people like us, to look after our sport and not just the land but the quarry itself. Have a bit of respect for our foxes and don't abuse them by hunting in the breeding season except when asked to deal with a vixen and cubs that are being a nuisance. Don't just go out looking for earths, slaughtering litter after litter of vixens and nursing cubs – that's not sport. Deal with them when they're being a nuisance to livestock but don't kill them just for the fun. We do sometimes get asked to deal with troublesome foxes during the breeding season, as a vixen with a litter of three-quarter grown cubs afoot, being taught all the tricks of the trade, is truly a pest.

As a boy, I remember going with my dad to see his prized golden duckwing game cock, who was running with 15 English game hens. On arriving at the game pens we found all the hens had been massacred – half plucked and torn bodies lay everywhere and my father's lovely game cock was lying in the grass with his head torn off. It was a horrible sight and one

Terriermen begin to dig down to the sound of the terrier baying.

97

which I shall always remember. I remember asking my father what could have done such a terrible thing. Foxes, my father and older brother said, taking a large chunk of bright red hair from beneath the wire the foxes had dug under. The terrible thing which always sticks in my mind is that they hadn't killed for food, just for fun – taking the heads off of each and every one. My father said it must have been a vixen that had taken this opportunity to teach her half-grown cubs killing and hunting tricks. With 15 chickens, a vixen and cubs in a pen, it must have been like shooting ducks in a barrel.

I think the most horrid sight that I have witnessed was at a riding school at Horsham in West Sussex. The riding school owners kept about 30 Rhode Island Red laying hens. The runs were about two feet off the ground, with wire mesh floors for easy cleaning. The foxes couldn't get into the runs so they had pulled the hens' feet through the wire mesh. Over 20 of the hens in the two runs had their feet and toes chewed off by the foxes – it was a horrid sight. My brother Robert, our friend Jimmy Peacock and I were shown the area of woodland where the earth which held the guilty foxes was believed to be. After searching the woodland for some 15 minutes, we came upon a small earth on a sloping bank. Lady was entered, Dusty was tied up and Blondy the lurcher put on a slip lead. Lady started baying straight away and bolted a three-parts grown cub, which Blondy caught after a very short run. But out of the same hole came an adult silver vixen. She ran down the bank and across the woodland. By the time I got Blondy's attention and Robert had got the, by now, very dead fox away from her, the silver vixen was long gone. Lady began baying and in just a few minutes we broke through, and found her with a large, red dog fox. He was quite a big fox and was putting up quite a fight. We used Toby the border dog to draw him with not too much fuss. Behind him were two more three-quarter grown cubs. We took four foxes that morning – four bright red ones – and the fifth, the lovely silver grey vixen got away. I think we must have done some good for our poultry-owning friends because they haven't had many fox attacks since.

I think silver foxes are becoming more and more common now, although the one that got away from us was almost certainly the mother of the cubs, none of the cubs we found in the earth were silver. Instead they had taken the colour of the dog fox. Although I have only seen two silver foxes in my district, reports of them from friends are quite common. I remember once catching a small dog fox in Henfield, Sussex,

Couples are an ideal way of tethering more than one terrier when out working.

that had one pure white front leg with black and tan spots scattered from the knee down to its toes. You will find foxes looking almost black but they are really all shades of red or dark brown. Most of the 'black' foxes I have seen were on the downs – I find that lowland foxes are a lighter colour. One black-looking fox I saw was on Steyning Downs: My father and I were on a hare coursing trip and as we walked down a large grass bank my dad put up two large foxes out of the long grass. One was a normal bright red fox and the other looked as if he was coal black from head to foot. We slipped the two lurchers on them. Mostly when two foxes get up together and make a run for it, they split up, but these two didn't, they ran side-by-side. As the lurchers speeded their way to them they disappeared along the grass bank. The dogs ran around sniffing the long grass. The foxes knew exactly where to go – they had disappeared down a very large badger sett that was obviously still holding badgers. It was a very large sett and it was late March, so the foxes were probably rearing their cubs in there along with the badgers.

The left terrier's missing eye is evidence of the dangers faced below ground.

I have seen these black-looking foxes quite a few times on the South Downs at Steyning and on Amberley Downs. There have also been reports of white badgers, albinos, and some people have told me about badgers that are almost totally ginger. To be quite truthful, I have only seen badgers that have been the traditional black and white, although on the downs they do seem to be more black-looking than the lowland badgers. I think this is to do with the sandy, clay and sandstone soil of the lowland earths, making the lowland badgers look more sandy and more reddy-brown than their downland relatives, who look a darker black and whiter. Nine out of ten downland setts are dug into the chalkland and I think the chalk keeps the badger's coat much cleaner, making his colours much darker and whiter. Some people say that there are different types of badgers, the downland ones being a larger, more fierce type of badger but, take it from me, badgers are badgers whether they live in the weald or lowlands, or high up on the downs. I have seen them in both places many, many times and haven't noticed any difference in size whatsoever.

I think the largest badger I have seen was some years ago in Henfield, Sussex, when we were moving a badger, or badgers, that were causing damage to livestock. The landowner had blamed foxes for killing some young goslings but when we searched the nearby land we found a badger sett which had traces of the goslings nearby. The landowner, now convinced that the badgers were guilty, didn't want them killed or harmed, just wanted them gone. So it was down to us to catch them. The next morning we arrived at the farm to be met by the landowner who said he had some more trouble in the night. He hadn't lost any more stock but there was a hole under the wire mesh fence, and some thick black and grey hairs had been caught in the wire. Mr Brock had been back for more late night snacks but was out of luck, what was left of the goslings were locked up safely and out of his reach. Geoff and I entered a Jack Russell dog that began to bay almost as soon as he went to ground. After moving around some two or three times, we finally got a steady mark on him and began to dig. We dug down about five feet and broke through to the dog, his badger was just around a bend. We opened up the pipe and got the first sight of our badger. We removed the Jack Russell and the badger came creeping out and was taken alive and unharmed. Then, from a little further up the pipe, came the biggest badger I have ever seen. His fur was puffed up, which made him look even bigger, but what was incredible was his length, and he wasn't hanging around. We tried to stop him but he was moving too fast and made his escape through the bramble bushes. We entered the dog again and took one more badger from the sett and released the pair suitably far from the farm. Our friend still had trouble from time-to-time and he said it was the one that got away coming back for revenge – more likely coming back for tasty goslings!

Poor old Mr Fox does get the blame for Brock's wrong doings sometimes. People don't think that our lovable old creature is capable of anything more than drinking milk sop from a saucer or eating blackberries from a bramble bush. They don't grow large canine teeth but have incredible biting power in their jaw and harmless vegetarians they certainly are not.

Badgers are more common now, in the 1980s, than they have ever been in the past. When we go out with our terriers we have more chance of finding badgers than foxes and it's most annoying, when you visit an old reliable fox earth, to find it has been taken over by badgers and so overnight has become out of bounds unless you want to risk ending up in court. If you have permission to hunt on some land and the landowner doesn't mind, it's a good idea to put down some artificial earths to encourage the foxes to breed and use them. If the earths on your land are very large then a few artificial earths will be useful to you. You can make them out of an old 45 gallon oil drum and a couple of ten inch land drain pipes. You can quite easily make one but do remember to slightly slope it so that it won't flood. Also make sure it is waterproof and dry, a little straw put in the den will help – after all, who wants to sleep in a wet or damp bed? Not a fox, that's for sure. We have bolted foxes from all sorts of places. In summer months, when the cubs are taken out into the corn, it's not uncommon to find foxes laying up in barns and hayricks and even in winter months I have come across a startled fox laying up between the straw bales. We have walked up to earths in late summer to find them laying out in the sun, sunning themselves. One earth along the main road, three miles from my house, is a one-holed earth in the bottom of an oak tree stump. Foxes can be seen sunning themselves by people driving past. The time I enjoy hunting most is after the foxes have had their cubs and reared them in as much peace as possible. And not with horse and hound, but as I said earlier with lurcher and terrier.

I have been hunting with a fox hunting pack. It was a very enjoyable day out, with lots of men and women riding some really good looking horses, about 25 couples of hounds and as many foot followers, of whom I was one. I didn't see any terriers get worked, I missed that part as by the time I got there it was all over and they had moved on somewhere else. They did kill a fox and it only took them four hours to catch it. You can take a lot more foxes with a little lurcher and terrier team; on the following Saturday I took two foxes in one hour.

There are so many different types of foxing lurchers to choose from. I use the same kind of lurcher for foxing as I do for hare coursing and that's a saluki/greyhound. I have other types or lurcher, Blondy is a saluki-greyhound/whippet-greyhound. This cross, in my mind, is the perfect hunting machine which will catch any British quarry day or night. Blondy is not only a good foxing bitch, she is an even better hare courser, killing

Black fell terriers have become very popular since the publication of Brian Plummer's The Fell Terrier.

three out of three hares in her youth almost every week on big hare coursing trips at Newmarket and Cambridge as well as taking many foxes bolted by terriers. She is also good on the lamp. Collie/greyhound, deerhound/greyhound and any other cross will catch foxes. We have on our smallholding two pure-bred border collies who can kill foxes. According to our neighbours, Badger and Tiger, as the two Collies are called, caught a large vixen in our neighbour's garden and killed it in his onion patch. The fox was feeding off scraps of food thrown down for the two collies by our friendly neighbours. When the collies arrived for their late-night snack they had a little extra. They made an awful mess of the fox, leaving holes in the carcass from nose to brush. But that doesn't mean that a collie is a natural fox killer. Most lurcher-types will catch foxes if they're fast and hard enough to. I have had some lurchers that looked like little whippets, that killed foxes. If you want an all round lurcher try a saluki-greyhound/whippet-greyhound or something along those lines and you won't go far wrong. My brother Robert has a pure-bred greyhound that's very good with terriers, isn't headstrong or bad with livestock, and is very well behaved. That's one in a hundred – most greyhounds will kill anything that moves, whereas a lurcher is much more sensible and a little more reserved. Our terriers get in enough danger underground without a working partner ready to sink his teeth into them if they look and smell a little bit like a fox when they come out of the ground.

Taking or despatching the fox

When you have dug to your terrier baying his fox 'what next?' the beginner would say. You need to know how to take him alive and unharmed, and also how to kill him humanely and quickly without causing unnecessary suffering. Firstly, if the fox is to be taken alive and to be released elsewhere: Your terrier has located his fox and has given a steady mark to his whereabouts by constantly baying at his fox, so you must dig down to him by listening to his voice coming up through the ground. Once you have broken through into the tunnel (it could be a very short dig of only a couple of feet or a long dig of a great many feet). Clear away all the loose soil around your terrier and block the tunnel behind your terrier to stop your quarry escaping. Your fox should be a few feet away in the direction your terrier is facing, backed up at the end of the tunnel.

Now to take him alive: if you have another terrier that will draw a fox then he can make the job a little easier by going up to the fox and grabbing him (or the fox will grab your dog). Then, by pulling him out, you can get a tight hold of the fox's neck. Get someone else to separate them. Once you have him in sight, remove your terrier, take your spade and push it along the side of the fox, putting him in between the side of the tunnel and the blade of the spade. Once his head is firmly in one place and he cannot turn around, slide your hand over or around him and get hold of his neck. Pull him out, taking hold of his back legs and keeping a firm grip of his neck. Only do this if you are on your own and have a box to transport your fox in. Transferring a fox from your hands to a sack without getting bitten can be a problem. But if you must – keep a firm grip of the fox's neck and, taking your sack, pull the sack around the fox's back legs and up over his body, but don't let go of his head until it is well into the sack. Once his head is inside the sack then it's the time to let go of his head and quickly double up the end of the sack. Tie it up firmly with string.

Once released into the sack the fox may give a few mad jumps and kicks, then go into a state of some kind of shock and lie very still. If you are moving foxes regularly it's best to use a box, something like a tea chest with a wire door let in to it. Sometimes when you dig up to a fox you can take him out by poking a stick in front of him so he can bite and lock on to it, thus pulling him out and taking him alive. I must confess that I haven't ever used this method but I do know several people who say that they have, and with great success.

But if you do not want to take him alive and merely want to kill the fox then this must be done quickly either by shooting him with a shotgun or by using .22 live ammunition such as is used in humane guns by vets, slaughterhouses and foxhunts. But you do need to acquire a special licence for these firearms. One thing that makes my blood boil is people taking potshots at foxes (and also badgers) with air rifles, .22s and 177s. It is a totally pointless, cruel and stupid thing to do. You have the tiniest chance of killing a fox with an air gun, in fact I don't know of anyone who has killed a fox with one. They are alright for shooting rats, rabbits and the odd rook or wood pigeon, for which I use them, but that is all. If you are not a shooting man, then to kill your fox you must give one very hard and sharp blow to the cranium. It may sound barbaric and cruel, but done properly your fox will not know what has happened.

The author handling a large dog fox which was taken alive to be released elsewhere.

The same fox ready for release in a safer place.

Tools of the Trade

Basically, the tools of the trade are you, your terrier and a spade and I wish it was that simple. We've discussed terriers so let's now look now at the spades. The type of spade is quite important, don't go for the light and thin wooden-shaft type, with a plastic handle. I have used this type quite a few times and they have always broken or been unsuitable. To do heavy digging, you need a heavy, stout spade, preferably with a thick, hard, wood shaft and handle and the blade should be longer than it is wide. Don't make the common mistake of getting a spade too heavy to carry on a long walk to an earth. At least one spade should be a teaspoon shape and half the length of your others – enabling you to use it in a tight place and ideal for tunnelling. Don't go for the home-made digging spade with the scaffold pole for a handle as it is useless. The one that I used was hard work, just to lift it, let alone dig with it. So, basically you need two strong digging spades, preferably one of them a strong teaspoon shape.

When you are working your terriers on downland or similar chalky/flinty soil it's a good idea to take along a good strong garden fork. Most downland earths are in chalkland and a garden fork is very handy to use to break up the chalk and flintstone. If you hit a flintstone layer, a sturdy garden fork is

107

A spade or spit is an essential tool for the terrierman.

just the thing to dig and break your way through it because they break up the stone and chalk much better than a spade. Also a fork is quite handy to put in front of your fox if you want a young unentered dog to have a look and learn to bay. It will stop your dog from tackling his quarry and getting himself unduly hurt, and stop your quarry from charging and getting away.

108

Sandstone can also be a problem and is very common in my district. One dig I will always remember was when we were about a mile from my house and had entered two border terriers in an earth on a small, sloping bank. We could hear the terriers baying and started to dig to them. They were about four feet down and the digging was quite good until we reached a layer of thick sandstone. When we tried to chop through it with our spades, it made our arms ring with the vibrations and we weren't

Tools of the trade: spades, nets, locaters and torch.

making much of an impression on it. In fact one of the spade ends started to bend, so it was decided to fetch an iron bar from the van. On my return with the iron bar, very little impact had been made on the sandstone ledge so we started to pound into the stone with the bar. After about 15 minutes of constant pounding we finally broke through it, and lifted the rubble out using our spades as levers. The stone was about two inches thick and four feet wide, and if it hadn't been for our iron bar I don't think we would have ever reached our terriers. They were another two feet down and by then had all but killed their fox. An iron bar is also very useful for using as a delving rod to find tunnels and pipes when searching for your terrier underground.

109

Next comes nets. Nets are very useful indeed, as we all know, especially if you don't have any running dogs. I find the five foot nylon net very satisfactory and cheaper than most. Don't over-stock with them, I have been hunting with men who have carried around 50–100 nets with them, why, I don't know, I never carry more than 10. Let's be honest, we rarely net more than five holes do we? Well, at least, I don't.

Then there are locators, or bleepers – a very important part of working a terrier today – and well worth investing in. I feel I should tell you, though, about the receiver collar, which takes hearing aid batteries. Once the batteries are screwed down in place, tape them up with electrical insulation tape as this will stop them from unscrewing underground, and thus preventing you finding your terrier. At the end of the day take the batteries out of the collar. The battery in the locator box is all right you just have to turn the dial on the box off but the collars are different. If the batteries are left in they will go on transmitting to most household electrical appliances, and by the time you need them again they will be useless.

Another thing to take with you, and can quite easily be carried in your coat pocket, is a torch. It doesn't have to be a big one, a small one is quite adequate. It is useful for shining in the tunnel when you break through and find your dog or your fox is a few feet further on, or when you break through to two pipes and your terrier's voice is coming out of both of them – a torch is handy to help you see where the breath and hair is coming from. Also, if the digging has to go into the night, a small torch is handy until a big one can be sent for.

There are so many items that can be useful on a hunting trip but if you tried to take them all you'd need a team of sherpas to carry them, so plan carefully before you go.

—6—

Ratting with Terriers

MIDGE MY OLD Jack Russell dog was a smashing little
ratter. He has passed away now but I have some
wonderful memories of ratting days with him. One
day we were ferreting an old dung heap with our small jill ferret
– a large ferret such as a big hob or a large liner is of very little
use as a rat-hunting ferret for they are far too large to hunt a rat
warren. Thus the ideal ratting ferret is a small or medium-sized
jill white or polecat ferret. I always prefer a white ferret to a
polecat, not for any better working preference but it's just that
you can see a white one more easily, but back to ferreting the
dung heap. We put our ferret in one of the well-trodden holes
and I waited on one side of the dung heap with Midge and my
brother was on the other side with his lurcher, Yeller. The next
thing we heard was rats squeaking, the little jill had obviously
made contact with her rats and from the sound of it was giving
them hell. Then the first one bolted and ran down the ditch with
Midge close on his tail, but not close enough, for the rat just
slipped back down the warren. So then I put Midge on a
slip-lead, as you would a lurcher. Another rat bolted and I
slipped Midge who caught it in a second. Before I could catch
hold of Midge another rat bolted and he caught that one as well.
The squeaking could be heard very clearly and I think the ferret

111

was accounting for more rats than the dogs were. Then a troop of about six half-grown rats came flying out. My brother slipped the lurcher who chopped and flicked his way through four of them before Midge killed the other two. So far nine rats had come out and eight were accounted for, as well as those that the ferret had despatched underground in the warren. When the little jill came out of the warren she had a lot of blood and quite a few bad bites on her face, but nothing too serious.

Two terriers killing a rat.

One chap recently approached me saying his smallholding was over-run by vermin (rats) and would I, if possible, rid his land of the creatures. The next Saturday, Geoff and I arrived at the smallholding. After a quick look around the buildings we only found a few signs of rats, nothing to justify the hoardes of rats we had been led to believe. Even the terriers, who are expert at finding rats, couldn't find anything worth our trip. To some people two or three rats seen running around feed sheds at night multiply in their minds, to become 60 or 70. Mind you, if any other animal – such as the fox or rabbit – was pursued and killed as often as the rat, they would certainly be extinct by now. When the good Lord handed out survival, the rat was definitely first in line.

Even on our smallholding, where there are dogs patrolling 24 hours a day, rats still find somewhere to hide and breed out of the terriers reach; but each morning one of the border collies has a rat or two lying in front of it. If any part of our smallholding is left unattended, particularly sheds with any-thing stored in them, the rats will take it over, literally overnight. In our chicken runs, where corn-feeders are tied up with string two feet off the ground, the full-grown rats will jump up and almost empty them by scratching the corn out of the feeder and onto the floor to the young rats too small, or too young, to make the two feet jump. Recently, while moving some cable which had been stored behind a chicken shed, Tess, my border/Russell bitch, started marking a small hole. When we had all but moved the cable (being between ferrets at that moment through trusting a lurcher too much with my ferrets – the lurcher killed them) I fetched a small spade and my old Staff bitch, Brock. So armed with two terriers, a saluki and a spade I started to follow the hole which Tess had marked. A very large rat suddenly bolted straight out in front of Ben, the saluki, who made quick work of it with just a quick chop and a flick. Just then two more rats, one big, one small, ran out straight through the legs of the dogs, myself, my brother Robert and Geoff. Lady Luck certainly shined on them that day as the dogs missed them. So did Geoff – about 25 times with a short-handled coal shovel – and they just disappeared down another hole under a shed. I wasted no time in blocking the exit hole they had bolted from. By this time Tess was digging frantically in the tunnel. We pulled her back and could just see a very scaly tail and two back feet. Tess dug in a little further and then made three short, sharp lunges and we heard a quick squeak – and out she pulled a very large buck rat, who wasted no time in biting Tess through the cheek. Tess has a great technique for killing rats, instead of shaking them to death as most dogs do, she just chews and crunches them. It's not always quick but it works well enough for her. She dealt with that one and straight away started scratching in the hole again. Then

113

a little more digging on my behalf and another scaly tail could be seen and Geoff decided, for some reason, that he wanted to pull it out by its tail. So with baited breath Robert and myself looked on, ready with the first aid kit. Geoff put his hand in the hole and got a firm grip on the end of the rat's tail, but it must have been a bit too firm a grip because two inches of the rat's tail broke straight off in Geoff's hand, to myself and Robert's disappointment. Tess pulled that one out as well and Brock and Tess finished it off. There were obviously more in there because Tess let Brock claim the kill and carried on digging in the hole, soon pulling yet another full grown rat out. To cut a long story just a bit short, Tess pulled 14 full grown rats out of the straight-through hole.

When the terriers are left loose to hunt around the smallholding they almost always end up digging and scratching

A Lakeland, border and Jack Russell digging for a rat at the base of a tree.

in some rat warren. We have in our kennel, at the moment, a Jack Russell-type terrier bitch who will not leave any place where there is a rat. One day, only a short time ago, we were working down the bottom of our smallholding when she started digging at a hole in a ditch. When I investigated I found she had uncovered a three-eyed rat warren. Not having the time to give her a hand I left her to enjoy herself with Beagle and Trixy, my border, giving her a hand along with the youngster of the moment, Tiny. After about five hours, when we had finished our work, we went to fetch the terriers. They had dug three feet into the bottom of the bank, and Beagle had dug about a foot into the top. There were seven or eight pieces of large rat lying around the bottom of the ditch. After getting a piece of stiff cable, I pushed it down the pipe Beagle had been digging at. I could feel something and as I gave one good shove, three more large rats met their death at the jaws of the little diggers, as I have now nicknamed them. They had been digging for five hours – digging and yapping non-stop.

I often stop and wonder, usually at the end of a day working terriers, where they get their drive from – that spirit which gives them the courage, endurance and stamina to go on all day without stopping, without even thinking of quitting or giving up, not letting anything get the better of them. That is how they are separated from the rest, that's why they are working terriers. Willing to tolerate a friendship with ferrets and polecats just for their love of working, some of my terriers behave with ferrets as if they are just a smaller version of another terrier. Tess and Beagle, when on ratting trips and even after killing four or five rats, will ignore the ferret when it emerges from the warren and it can walk freely amongst them, in complete ease.

A lot of people have a great deal of trouble finding sufficient ratting for their terriers, but if you think of the most likely places to look or as a terrierman said to me once, think if you were a rat where would you live in your area – anywhere there's food enough and somewhere they can sleep and breed. The first places to try is all the local farms and smallholdings in your district. Not all farmers are keen on poisoning rats, not through any sympathy for the rats but through fear of their own stock coming into contact with the deadly poison. To be honest I am not keen on using poisons, only where I cannot ferret or use any other means to shift them, then poison has to be used. If poison has been used on any premises prior to ferreting, don't put your ferret in because of the rats that have died from poisoning. Any ferret finding a dead rat will be too quick to take advantage of a free meal, but the free meal will be a deadly one. Any rat dying of poison is indeed poison itself. And the same goes for terriers.

A jill ferret keeping a tight hold on her catch.

My old terrier, Midge, spent his days finding and killings rats and eating them. Practically every rat that he found and caught, he ate. He lived until he was 15 years old, and died in my arms one morning. Throughout his life he killed a great number of rats, rabbits and fox, although his main job was ferreting. The only foxes he killed were those he found himself, but despite all the bites he had from rats, and he was always in contact with them, he never got any kind of disease from them, the likes of which have killed a great number of dogs. If any of my other terriers kill a rat, they will carry it around, proudly showing off their prize for all the world to see, but will not eat it. Tess, the grand-daughter of Midge, is the only terrier that will eat a rat, perhaps inherited through her grand-father.

Even the best planned ratting days can go wrong. Recently we left to do some ratting on a tip, 18 miles from my home. Geoff, our good friend Steven Guy and I met at the tip looking forward to a day's ratting and hoping to take some ratting photos for this book. We visited the first lot of warrens along a large ditch we'd found a week earlier, and to our disappointment our rat-filled ditch was now water-filled through two days of torrential rain. Our next spot, on the other side, was just as useless because several tons of wood had been tipped on the warrens. By now things were looking bad, but things were to get worse. Tess marked a warren which on our last visit had been a heap of 45 gallon oil drums, but topsoil had been tipped on them and it was now an ideal place for rats to live, but not a good place to ferret. We have lost some good ferrets in bad places like this before and we weren't about to risk another one. It would have been too easy for my ferret to enter the warren and drop into one of the old oil drums underground. Then to round off the day nicely, it poured down with rain. So you see reader, everyone has disaster days.

A new method of rat control that I have been using recently has proved quite efficient. For about two weeks I have been flushing rats from around the chicken houses at night and shooting them with a 16 bore as they run across the stable walls. I have been bagging five or six a night but now they choose to take their chances on the ground with the terriers rather than with the 16 bore. My hunting partner, Geoff, prefers using the .22 air rifle instead of the 16 bore which reduce the rat to just a blood-stained patch of fur on the stable wall. A bit gory but it's another way of dealing with rats.

Cage traps can be effective but I find that after using it in one spot for a couple of days, the rats seem to get wise to them and stay away from them. I set a catch live cage-trap recently, baited with some corned beef, and one of the collies picked up the trap and carried it off, and that was the last we ever saw of it. Those kind of traps are priced at about £10, so the next one will be nailed to the ground. The rats on our smallholding seem to get wise to a trap – once a few rats have been caught, they seem to leave a trap well alone, no matter what the bait may be.

One of the most efficient ratters that I have had the pleasure of seeing work, was my sister's border terrier bitch, Blue. Blue was litter sister to my first border terrier bitch, Dusty. Blue was a little bigger and a bit less restrainable – by that I mean she would fly into any other terrier which so much as growled at her. She never went to ground but rats and rabbits were all grist to her mill. If a rat was behind some straw bales, or in a hay-rick, she wouldn't stop searching or scratching and pulling with her jaw at whatever was between them until it moved or was torn up. I never saw her beaten to the kill when ratting. I have flushed rats out of hiding places quite a few times to five or six terriers, all of which were fast killers, but if Blue was on the team she would beat them to it every time.

One night, while hunting with a pack of about twelve dogs, including Blue, I flushed a rat out from of an old heap of lorry tyres. The pack gave chase but Blue was there three or four seconds in front of the rest of them, beating a mixture of collies, alsatians, lurchers and terriers. She always seemed to know where a rat was going to bolt from and she never wrongly marked a spot where rabbit or rat might be hiding. If she paid a lot of attention to a spot you could bet your shirt there was a rat or rabbit hiding there.

While out one day doing a spot of bush hunting for rabbits with lurchers and terriers, Blue marked a single hole in some quite thick cover and started yapping and digging. She wouldn't stop and come when she was called to move on so we left her and worked the rest of the surrounding bushes and scrubland for about half an hour. On our return to Blue she had dug out a large doe rabbit which was definitely, by now, dead and Blue was tucking into a tasty meal of new born baby rabbits. It's not something I like to see but it was late March and probably the first litter of the year, and I was unlucky enough to come across them. I have no doubt in my mind if she had been introduced to earth work she would have taken to it like a duck takes to water, she was that kind of dog, always keen and eager to search out every nook and cranny she came across. She certainly caught great numbers of rats during the years she spent with us.

This demon rat-hunter was no early starter, she didn't kill anything until she was at least two years old. In fact when she was a one-year-old she would just look at a rat with no more than just a little curiosity. Once when moving some pigs, a rat ran out from some feeding troughs and ran almost between Blue's legs, and all she did was look at it. When shown a ferret she would just shy away from it, and then one day something inside her head clicked and she would fight and kill anything, even ferrets. If left alone she would even try and scratch out a ferret from its cage.

Border terrier team searching a rock pile for rats.

Another terrier which is quite an accomplished ratter is also owned by my sister. Amy is a red Stafford bitch only about 28 pounds in weight and a very fast mover. She's probably a little of the old-fashioned type and is the grand-daughter of the famous Satan's Master, a great Staffordshire Bull Terrier dog whose stud fee stood at £500 to well bred Stafford bitches only. Phil Drabble, in his wonderful book '*Of Pedigree Unknown*' said that the Staffords of that day still had the agility and were still of the type to rat with a good degree of success, but a lot of Staffords and English Bull Terriers of today are much too big and heavy for dealing with rats bolted by ferrets. Although the dogs would probably be willing enough, the thick cloddy shape they are taking on now would definitely go against them in the field. There are still strains of Staffordshire Bull Terriers which are suitable for work but you will most certainly not find one at any dog show of any kind today. Amy and her aunt, Brock, are the only Staffords I have seen which will work with ferrets and other terriers day and night without fighting, even in the heat of the hunt when even the most placid of terrier's tempers get high. Amy and Brock will keep a cool head and their minds stay on their rats, and not on their fellow terriers.

Whilst writing this book we tried to take some action photos of some ratting but after all was said and done none of us are photographers. There's one photo that I really wish we could have got, but the photos I tried to take of it just turned out to be a series of blurs and nothing recognisable. We were ratting down our lane and hadn't had much luck when I flushed a large rat from under some old wire. The rat made a dash for it but Beagle flicked it and Trixy caught it and flicked it again when it bit her. A third dog, Blondy the lurcher, struck it, picked it up and when it bit her she tossed it five feet into the air. The rat landed on the ground, let out a quick squeak, ran for cover and escaped. The rat had been through the mouths of two terriers and a lurcher and had still got away. The only way anyone would truly be able to believe the incident is if I could have caught the moment on a video camera. It would have been something you most certainly wouldn't get fed up watching.

I know of some terriers which will kill foxes without thinking twice about the consequences, and then shy away from a rat. It sounds funny but a friend of mine recently had some trouble with rats and, one morning, found one of the troublesome rats in a feed barrel. Being the owner of a very hard black and tan lakeland dog and an equally-hard black patterdale dog, he thought he'd have no trouble and tossed them straight into the feed bin with the most certainly doomed rat. It wasn't to be so; when the feet of the two hard-as-iron terriers hit the bottom of the corn bin, the rat ran around their paws and the terriers jumped out as fast as they were put in. Their bewildered owner tried them back at the rat, one at a time, but they were terrified of the rat and were having nothing to do with it. Two terriers who would most certainly kill any fox, were afraid of a tiny little rat. I have had hard, fox-killing lurcher dogs, big and tough enough to kill a fox single-handed, but show them a rat and they'd become whining cowards with their tails between their legs. Yet some dogs will not tackle a fox but will kill rats for fun.

A Jack Russell digging for a rat.

Tiny, our young pup from Tess and Beagle's mating, is a real sod for ferrets. From a very early age she has gone mad at them, yapping, barking and snapping at my ferrets. So now, at the time of writing, she is seven-months-old and cannot be trusted for one moment with any ferrets at all. It seems it's a bad year for breaking puppies to ferrets because Bingo, our new lakeland/patterdale-type terrier, is ten-months-old and will not tolerate the presence of any ferret or polecat that comes within her sight. So for ferreting rats Bingo and Tiny are most definitely out. I prize my ferrets too highly to take a chance on them getting killed by one of my terriers.

Rats often take refuge in drains, land-drains and sewage drains, but these places are definitely not to be ferreted. Well, not unless you have an unlimited number of ferrets, for we have lost quite a few ferrets in drains, to our discredit. So now we leave drains well alone. Some rats have recently taken up residence right underneath the top ratting terriers' kennels. The cheek of these rodents will never cease to amaze me but at least I can solve that problem. Once, last winter, when kennelling our Rottweiler closer to the boundary of our land, we moved her old kennel only to find four large rats had started living under there. The Rottweiler is not a bad hand at killing rats and she dealt with two of these four in not too much time. A gun always comes in handy when ratting, especially if you go ratting at night. Take last night, for instance; at about 11 o'clock I went to lock up the young game birds we had bred this year, for we let all the young pullets and stags run loose all day and shut them in at night to protect them from foxes, of both the two-legged, and four-legged kinds. On my rounds I took along, as always, Tess, the two collies and Blondy. There were hardly any rats out, we only saw five and the dogs killed three of them. On our return I saw one of the biggest rats that I have ever seen. At first glance it looked like a rabbit, then it hopped under our telephone box, which stands on a large forklift palette. I shone my torch under there and could see the giant sitting between two wooden blocks. There was no way Tess could get him, or any other one of the dogs. First I thought I would get my ferret, but the thought of using a ferret at turned 11 o'clock at night didn't appeal to me, so I fetched my .22 air pistol and, kneeling down I shone the torch to where I had last seen him, and there he was. By now he had turned round and his large behind was facing me. I shot him where it hurts. That didn't kill him but it made him run out into the waiting jaws of the border collies. If it wasn't for my trusty air pistol I don't think I would have moved him for quite a while.

Whatever you use for ratting, most methods are good enough. Most rat-hunting men swear by their own personal methods. As long as a method flushes out rats for your terrier to catch, it's good enough. One method of bolting rats for terriers that I used recently, was flooding them out with a water pump. We were pumping out a large water container holding around ten thousand gallons of water and the outlet pipe was pushed firmly down a large rathole. It was quite a large rat warren about 30 yards along a dry ditch. Needless to say it wasn't dry for long. It wasn't until water was running out of half of the holes that the rats started bolting. It was, up-to-date, one of the most efficient ways we have used to flush a great number of rats all at once; because it seemed all the rats were bolting at the same time, big ones, small ones, the whole colony seemed to bolt. The terriers were having a field day, not to mention one saluki and two saluki/greyhound pups. The pure saluki nailed just about as many as did the terriers. All-in-all I think we bolted about 30 rats and killed 23, plus the ones that Tess ate. The pump we used was much higher pressured than any ordinary garden hosepipe. In fact, I do not recommend using a garden hose to flood out rats from their warrens because there just isn't enough pressure to flood the warren out. The water would just soak away into the ground.

So now you have an idea of the different methods and ways of bolting and killing rats. Remember, they may be on the bottom of the hunting quarry list but they are still legal quarry for our terriers. So try, and I know it's hard, to treat them with just a little bit of respect. Good ratting.

Nightime Ratting with Terriers, Lurchers and Airguns

Most of our rat-hunting sport comes from hunting at night, with a CTF fieldsports rabbiting lamp, a .22 air rifle and a pack of dogs, consisting of Brock and Amy, two Staffordshire Bull Terriers; Badger and Tiger, two border Collies; Tess, Beagle, Trixy and Tammy, a mixture of border terriers and Jack Russells; Blondy and Whippy, the two lurchers and sometimes Ben, the saluki, tags along. It sounds quite a mixed up bunch of all sorts and that's just what it is. But Oh Boy! Can they catch rats.

One night we decided to gather up the rat-pack and deal with the rat problem around the stables, chicken sheds and cable yard. Geoff and I started at 8 o'clock one night in November.

Geoff was armed with a stick and our rabbiting lamp, and I had my .22 air rifle and our hunting rat-pack was running loose. We started by hunting the stableyard and Tiger started marking at the back of our horsebox where a rat had taken

The Drak Pack making short work of a rat.

refuge between the twin wheels. Geoff shone the lamp in there and a large grey rat could be seen hunched up, out of the dogs' reach. By this time all the dogs were pushing around the wheels of the lorry, so I slipped the airgun barrel between the wheels and with one shot dealt with the first rat of the night. Next, all the dogs started hunting around some old tin sheets. Geoff shone the lamp and I kicked over the sheets, four rats made a dash for cover. I don't know who killed what first, but Blondy flicked one up in the air and the two collies and the bull terriers caught it, and that was the end of that. The other three were accounted for by Trixy and Whippy before the rest could get there. After searching the rest of the yard, we found nothing and started to search the stable area but the first six stables drew

124

a blank. In the seventh, Geoff shone the lamp in and, out of the horses' feed-bowl, came a gang of half-grown grey rats, about six of them. As soon as they settled on the rafters I shot the first one and the rest scattered off in all directions. 'Should have had a double-barrel 12 bore,' Geoff said 'would have got the lot then with one shot,' Geoff tends not to be very thrilled with the thrill of the chase. That's no so bad, we do make a good team. We tried the next stable and I shot another two rats. The dogs were getting a little frustrated with only hearing my airgun go off and then seeing a dead rat come flying over the door.

We had noticed that there were not many rats about and Geoff said, 'Let's do the little hazel cock's shed next. I filled his self-feeder up with a half hundredweight of wheat today.' We skipped the lane, cable yard, the other small chicken pens, the back of the stables and the old sheds and made our way to the large brick-built shed where the hazel cock and his harem of Indian game-hens were kept. The only way in is through the wire-mesh door and as we flicked the beam through the door about 20 rats ran across the floor, away from the self-feeder. They all seemed to huddle under the nesting boxes. Geoff said, 'let all the dogs in and I will move the nest-boxes over.' 'No, wait,' I said, 'just let Amy in and then you can move the nest-boxes.' The rest of the dogs were getting very excited and we were making quite a racket, with their whining and yapping, as Geoff slipped through the door. Or should I say tried to slip through the door as I opened the door about 14 inches wide and Geoff weighs in at about 19½ stone. It was a very tight fit. Anyway, he got in there and without letting the Drak pack in, as they were nicknamed, I pushed Amy into him and Geoff let her loose on the floor. She immediately started scratching under the nest-boxes. Geoff said, 'Give me another dog, I bet there's a lot more rats under these boxes. Give me Beagle, let's see if he can kill rats as quickly as they say his ancestors can.' I originally bought Beagle from Harold Hobson-Walker, but Beagle's sire is Brian Plummer's Vampire, a famous ratting dog owned by a famous rat-hunting man. I passed Beagle into Geoff and then waited for the fun to start. Geoff quickly turned over the nest-boxes and 25 rats ran in all directions. The little red Stafford bitch, Amy, moved quickly into action and started killing rats, big ones, small ones and all sized rats. Killing them

125

with a powerful crushing bite and sometimes a back and neck-breaking flick, pounding her rats against her red cheeks, snapping and biting rats as she came to them. Beagle was doing very well, catching them as fast as he could but taking a little longer to kill them than Amy. Nevertheless, he got the job done. As they went through the mob, those left were trying to run up the walls only to be dealt with by Geoff and his stick. After a few minutes there didn't seem to be any life left in any of the rats and the score, as near as we could reckon it, was fourteen to Amy, seven to Beagle and four to Geoff, and none got away. We tried the rest of our ratting places but never saw a thing. Once we had kennelled the dogs we totalled up our catch. We were quite pleased with ourselves – 32 rats in only two hours of hunting with the Billingshurst drak-pack.

I must admit my fondest memories of ratting are with my old Russell dog, Midge. Ferreting the old dung heaps, where litters had been bred for years and which harboured hoards of rats and sometimes even rabbits. Rabbits also fall victim to the drak-pack. Even the terriers, which are my finest foxing dogs, when with the rest, kill and worry rabbits with the best of them. I expect I will come under criticism for allowing my working terriers to do this but, then again, it's up to us all how we work our terriers and it's very rare for one of my terriers to bay, or stick to, a rabbit underground. To say my terriers have never worried rabbits underground would be a lie and a terrier should know the difference when he goes foxing, ratting or even rabbiting. Which reminds me of a funny story you might like to hear: While out foxing one day we dug three feet to a friend's young terrier and found it baying a rabbit. We were all cussing and cursing the terrier for its bad habit and making us dig for nothing, when another friend of mine looked up and said, 'Well at least you can eat a rabbit, you can't eat a fox.'

—7—

Not Only Earth Dogs

S WELL AS having a great deal of courage and gameness to work fox in the depths of the earth, a working terrier has other uses. I know the purists will jump up and down in temper and say a terrier's job is to work foxes, and only killing a few rats is otherwise allowed, but a terrier can be a great little all round sportsman. My terriers work all sorts of places in summer and winter, not only on foxing trips but on hare coursing trips as well. When the corn first gets cut and the straw is still in layers on the stubble, our hare coursing season officially starts. You can walk across a lot of hares lying under the straw and that's when a terrier with a good nose is very handy.

Dusty, my old border bitch, was quite a good hare finder. On many a day's coursing, mine or my father's eyes would be on her watching her little red-brown carrot-shaped tail wagging faster and faster as she got on a scent that was getting stronger and stronger. Then suddenly, as if popping up like a Jack-in-a-box, a hare would fly off its seat like a brown rocket, leaving my little border terrier standing. But, when we slipped one of our lurchers on the hare whilst the course was going on, it was great to see how many corners the little border terrier bitch would cut and the short cuts she would take whilst trying to keep up with the hare and its pursuer. Once the kill was made it wasn't that long before she was there, but if the hare was lost and the lurcher was marking a hedgerow or some thicket, Dusty would soon pick up the scent of the hare and flush him out, to run again or, if luck was on her side, catch it in the thicket. That was very rare indeed, for a terrier to catch a hare on its own.

One enjoyable afternoon's hare flushing, was when my father and I went hare coursing on Amberley marshes, which is a large open marsh and grassland, criss-crossed with dykes and ditches. It holds great numbers of wildfowl, and a large number of hares which we exercised regularly. In the middle of the marshes was a large clump of reeds and water rushes, and the hares, when hard-pushed, made straight for this thicket which was like an impregnable fortress to any lurcher which tried to follow them in. The thicket was situated where all the ditches and dykes seemed to meet or cross to get to each other, in a complex series of dykes and ditches. On this particular day we arrived at the marshes around midday, with four running dogs, more than we usually took and, of course, my inseparable companion Dusty, the border terrier. Off we went, walking the fields with two lurchers on slips, and the two young lurchers running loose to learn a little self-taught hunting, by scent and sight. We walked most of the marshes without seeing so much as a sign of a hare, but as we walked nearer the marsh clump our first hare came in sight and the young lurchers were off in a second, only to lose their hare in the clump or thicket. We put two more hares up which made straight for the thicket.

We walked around the thicket to walk back up to the car but Dusty picked up the scent of a hare and disappeared into the clump. She began working the thick cover and soon got on to the hare because she began baying and yapping quite strongly. After giving chase around the thicket, for some five minutes, a hare came darting out and made a dash for the large riverbank nearby. Two more hares decided to leave their grassy fortress and we got a run on one of them which was promptly caught and killed. Dusty was coming out on a scent and going back in, throwing her tongue like any beagle pack out hare hunting. After about one hour in the thicket, Dusty was covered in a brown, filthy sludge from the ditch and smelling as if she had been in a cesspit, so I called her out and off we went on our way back to the car.

Walling in Yorkshire, using terriers to detect the rabbit.

Lucas, in his masterpiece on working terriers *Hunt and Working Terriers*, has a photo of a pack of pedigree smooth fox terriers hunting and driving like hounds. I can't quite see what

129

they have killed but I believe it to be a hare. Terriers have such a wide range of sporting qualities that they can adapt and be used at almost any sport. One photo in particular in Lucas's book, is of a pack of Jack Russells, owned by Major K. A. C. Doig, which killed a jackal after hunting it for 65 minutes. The terrier is quite a remarkable little dog, being able to hunt anything from hedgehogs to foxes. One of my uncles trains his terriers to sniff out and find hedgehogs. A terrier can also be a first class ferreting dog.

Another quarry the terrier has adapted to, and learned to hunt, is the coypu. It looks rather like a large rat, but doesn't have his small lookalike's courage, I'm glad to say. Although naturalists say that they are mainly vegetarian, they do have a large pair of gruesome looking front teeth, which friends who have hunted them tell me can break off into a dog if it bites one. They are not common where I live and although there have been reports of them near Bognor Regis, I have never seen any myself. From friends' reports, the ones that they have hunted have been very poor sport – not giving much of a fight and when hard-pushed through water, make a pitiful humming noise. To be truthful, I have never been coypu hunting with terriers, and from what I have heard I don't think I would enjoy hunting them.

Another quarry our terriers have learnt to hunt is the mink, although it sometimes baffles me what some of my friends say about entering their terriers to a mink. All the minks that I have seen run to ground by mink hounds have been run into either rabbit holes, small drains or some large entangled tree roots, beside a river or stream. My local mink hound pack are the Wealden Mink Hounds, who run some really big patterdales who originate from the Duke of Beaufort's fox hounds. The terriers, bred by Stewart Adset, are by far the biggest patterdales that I have seen, but the pack do catch quite a few mink. I have hunted mink along miles of riverbank and in the time I have been doing it have only caught a couple of brace of mink. My terriers do enjoy it, and our kills have been in rather large reed and grass clumps on riverbanks. Mink do have a vicious bite and are harder and faster than any ferret I have ever seen.

Most terrier books will advise you to enter your terrier to stoats and weasels before foxes, but I have hunted a great deal of stoat-infested woodland with terriers and guns, and have shot far more than my terriers can catch. Around our smallholding the terriers seem to turn up a weasel now and again but the stoats seem to elude us. If I had to enter my terriers to stoats before fox, I think my dogs would be too old to go to ground by the time I could catch one, unless it was with a 12 bore.

Terrier racing at shows provides dogs and owners with a bit of excitement.